I0541948

A Lifetime with Death

By: Lindsay Fernandez, LMHC

Copyright © 2024
Life After Loss, LLC

All rights reserved. No part of this book may be reproduced, stored,
or transmitted by any means – whether auditory, graphic, mechanical,
or electronic – without written permission of the publisher, except in the case
of brief excerpts used in critical articles and reviews. Unauthorized reproduction
of any part of this work is illegal and punishable by law.

ISBN: 979-8-218-48003-5

Because of the dynamic nature of the internet, any web addresses or links in
this book may have changed since publication and may no longer be valid.
The views expressed in this work are solely those of the author and do not
necessarily reflect the opinions of the publisher, and the publisher hereby
disclaims any responsibility for them.

Bird House Publishing rev date 9/22/24

*****Note to Readers: This book references subjects that may cause
strong emotional reactions, including mental health struggles,
family dysfunction, and death. This work is intended to increase awareness,
decrease stigma, and inspire public discourse on these subjects but may not be
considered appropriate for all audiences.*****

Dedication:

To my beautiful mother, I will forever love you in this lifetime and the next. And to my amazing brothers, Raymie & Raylin, you guys have been right by my side throughout the rollercoaster of life; together, we are three souls and one heartbeat.

Contents

Foreword written by
ALICIA HARRIS-FERNANDEZ

Compassionate. Selfless. Empathetic.

These are just a few words I would use to describe Lindsay when we first met back in 2005, and they've never rang truer than today. Reading her new memoir, "A Lifetime with Death," gave me the opportunity to learn about her life through her eyes, through her pain, and through her grief.

"A Lifetime with Death" takes the reader on a rollercoaster. Just when you think it's over, there's another steep drop not too far away. From being exposed to violence, prescription drug addiction, and mental illness by her mother, Samantha, Lindsay's memoir captures her truth. A truth that, despite knowing her for 19 years, I knew little about. In spite of all of the unfathomable experiences she went through and the difficulty she faced trying to navigate a tumultuous mother-daughter relationship, she never victimized herself or subscribed to the "woe is me" club, even when justified. Instead, through her grief of her mother's unexpected passing in 2011, she reflects and puts herself in her mom's shoes and thinks about how she could've done more to help her. She is careful not to villainize her mother but instead memorializes her in a gracious way that shows the audience the very real ups and downs of mental illness. And to be honest, I admire her even more because of it.

Introduction to

BOOK ONE

Hello, and welcome to the story of my life! You chose to read this book because you are either a family member or friend who wanted to continue to support me in my endeavors or perhaps you are a stranger who saw my title "A Lifetime with Death - Book 1" and wondered, *What is that about?* Whatever your reasons may have been for selecting to read this book, I thank you. In my journey, I have received unconditional support and love from many people who gave me the push I needed, especially when I just wanted to throw in the towel. Life can feel and become exhausting, and yet we continue; someway, somehow.

My journey in writing this book has been a long one. It has been dreadful at times, yet reflective. I decided to write this book at the age of 15. By that point, I had lived through and experienced a world of pain that I didn't know how else to express. I looked at my life and the lives of those around me and realized that mine was different. My experiences, my household, and my feelings were not the same as those of my friends. Often, I remember feeling worried more than anything. I worried for my mom. I worried about school. I worried that I wasn't doing my best. Worry took over my ability to feel relaxed. It took away my ability to enjoy the moment and simply have fun. Early on, I learned how to gauge the temperature of the room any time I was with a group of people. It was almost as though once I noticed the energy in the room, I felt responsible for maintaining "the good vibes" within the group. If anyone was unhappy, I almost immediately tried to figure out what was wrong with them and how I could help them.

For a long time, I didn't know what to make of my constant worry, so I silenced it. I figured if I didn't say the things I was feeling and experiencing out loud, then I could be just like my friends and, with time, might even start feeling like them. I quickly realized that just wasn't going to work. Life would definitely not let me off the hook that easily. Realizing my need for expression, I put pen to paper and wrote my first 15 pages, and after that, I put it away for almost another 15 years. But even as I had stopped writing this book, it was always in the back of my mind. It has been on my mind like a pending task that I have avoided at all costs until now.

It was January 2020, when I was 29 and speaking to a close mentor and guide. I decided to pick this book back up and finally write the damn thing. Rosa, a very special person to me, knew that this would be no easy task and developed an intimate mastermind group to help motivate me to follow through with writing it. It's sometimes so easy for me to procrastinate when it comes to achieving my goals because I usually find myself so busy supporting everyone else that I barely have enough fuel for myself.

I started with the mindset that I wanted the book to continue being about my life, experiences, reflections, and truth. I also wanted this book to honor the memory of my mother, who has played a significant role in my life and work. Much of this, and everything I do, is with her in mind and at heart. I wanted to establish that sentiment in this book and decided to make the book three parts, with a total of twenty-two chapters, because her birthday was on March 22. Three parts, 22 chapters. Are you catching my drift now? Always look for the hidden messages with me, and you'll see the true story.

For months, I juggled my job, graduate school, the gym, a semi-decent social life, and writing this book. There were times when I thought to myself, *What's the point?* I had so many fears. What if I had finished the book but didn't feel anything? What if I was not expressing myself clearly, and my message was lost to the reader? These doubts and fears occupied me many times, so this mastermind group was great as it allowed me the space to express my fears and learn that others struggled with insecurities as well.

I continuously put time pressure on myself, thinking that this book should have been finalized by December 2020 because otherwise, it would just fall back in between the cracks, like it did many years before. I felt defeated whenever I didn't meet a deadline I had set for myself. I often criticized myself for taking more than 15 years to finish a book.

"This is my book! It should be easy to write!" I would often tell myself. I was supposed to get in, write about my experiences, and get out immediately. Why has it taken me this long?

The truth is that every time I began to write about my life, my experiences, and my feelings throughout these chapters, I re-entered a world that I didn't want to remember. I didn't want to return to the places I had lived through because I was confronted with the unprocessed feelings and thoughts from those experiences. The realizations that came to me fifteen years after the fact were difficult and painful, yet they somehow managed to provide me with some level of acceptance and peace for the situation. Peace, not because I had magically forgotten about the pain but because I saw that, at the end of the day, everyone in my life, including myself, did the best they could with what they were given.

I also remember having a hard time initially with some of the feedback I received during the mastermind sessions. Normally, before our calls, I would submit my chapters to Rosa and Gladys, the other members of the group. After reviewing it, they would provide me with their suggestions, thoughts, and overall feedback. I've always considered myself receptive to constructive feedback, but for some reason, I found myself resisting it this time around. I often found myself defending what I wrote and why because it's all my perspective, but I realized that if I weren't open to suggestions, I wouldn't be able to move forward with completing this book in any meaningful way. Instead of pouting and leaving the mastermind group offended, thinking that my friends had no idea what the hell they were talking about, I decided to have a one-to-one with myself and try to understand why I was constantly in this literary fight with people I call my friends.

I sat with myself long enough to realize that I wasn't used to being vulnerable or sharing my honest, true story, so when I did (in the form of this book), the critiques felt like an attack and maybe, in some way, invalidation. I remember countless occasions when my parents would tell my brothers and me that the things that happened at home stayed at home, so going against what I was taught and essentially making my private life public was a big deal.

Telling my story the unfiltered version was like walking into foreign territory. I didn't know how to do it, but I knew I had to figure out a way. Thanks to Rosa and Gladys showering me with support, love, and empathy, I slowly shifted from writing from my comfort zone to writing from the heart. Through the process, they validated me and the content I wrote, no matter how intense it might have been. Being "too much" has been an adjective that some people have verbalized to me when hearing bits and pieces of my life, and now that I am thinking about it, my parents seemed to support this same notion with their whole mindset of "what happens at home stays at home" motto. In the end, no one wants to be judged, and I didn't want you, the reader, to see my mom as the "Big Bad Wolf" or to see me in any unfavorable light, but Rosa and Gladys were instrumental in helping me remain honest and truthful, even when the taste wasn't palatable.

Writing this first book has been an intense journey for me. I have cried more times than I could count. I have laughed. I have reflected and welcomed the processing of my experiences and emotions. I haven't quite made it to the "other side" of grief, whatever that means, but I will keep you posted on my findings.

For the Lindsay 2.0 out there who may be struggling with your life and your experiences and feel alone in this world, I am here to wrap you in my loving embrace and let you know that you will survive. You will overcome this. You will not feel this way forever. You are not alone. And you are loved. Forget about how people tell you to live. Live your truth! Don't rush the process. Set your own standards and trust that you have all the answers you are looking for.

I thank you for joining me in my journey. Welcome to my story!

Chapter 1

THE DAY
WE ALL DIED

April 6, 2011 – The date that ended my life...her life. I remember this day as if it were yesterday. It started off as an average day.

It was about 10:00 am, and as usual, I dragged myself out of bed to get ready to go to work. I was living in New Rochelle, NY, at the time and was grateful for the peace and quiet surrounding the town. What I wasn't grateful for was the public transportation schedule; buses typically ran once every thirty minutes, which in turn meant that if I missed a bus (which I often did), I would either have to wait 30 to 35 minutes for the next bus and risk being late to work, or I could just walk it out and get to work on time. I typically chose to walk it out and call it a day.

I worked at a real estate company and was also a student at Iona College. Because Iona was a straight shot to my job, my co-workers sometimes spotted me walking and offered me rides down the avenue. While there were times I accepted the ride, other times I truly preferred to simply walk, as this gave me time to be and not think about anything while listening to music on my headset.

April 6, 2011, was supposed to be quite the normal, uneventful day, except that I had been counting down towards this day for quite some time. It was one of my very good friend's birthdays, and normally, to add excitement to the upcoming day, I would hold a countdown on Facebook until the day finally arrived. Five more days…4 more days…3 more days…2 more days…1 more day. Little did I know that I was counting down to something more life-changing than I could've ever imagined.

Prior to this day April 3rd, to be exact I had mentioned to my boyfriend at the time that I had been experiencing several restless nights; three, to be exact. There was truly nothing out of the ordinary that was stressing me out to the point of losing sleep. My life was going okay, and I was at peace. I didn't think much about it and just dismissed it since there were no valid reasons for my recent case of insomnia. The next day, my boyfriend at the time (yes, I will continue to say "at the time" just to be clear, hahaha) needed a memory stick that was in the Wii gaming system that he had previously gifted my mom. He drove me to her home for a quick visit to pick up the memory stick. I went inside the apartment that I once considered home for the first 18 years of my life. This apartment gave me some of my best memories but also some of my worst. I knocked on the door, and my mom opened it. I went inside and greeted her. Everything was very casual and nonchalant.

I went to where the Wii gaming system was, grabbed the memory stick, and said, "Okay, Mom, I have to go now." Before I could reach the door, my mom asked if we could exchange phone cases, as she liked mine. My mom and I typically exchanged items with each other and eventually returned them. Sometimes! I said, "Sure," and she switched the cases. As I walked towards the door, I turned to her, and she looked at me and said, "I love you." To most people, a parent saying "I love you" is normal, but after my parents divorced, anything having to do with showing affection of any sort was out the window. For a long time, we simply co-existed as a family and became people of few words. The few times my mom told me she loved me, I would normally respond with a sarcastic remark, which was code for "I love you too."

However, on this day, I didn't feel like using sarcasm and instead said the words back. "I love you too, Mom." After the exchange, I looked at her and asked if everything was okay because something seemed off. I couldn't pinpoint anything specific, but I had this feeling that something wasn't right. After assuring me three times that she was fine, I decided to let it go, hugged her, and took one last look at her from the entrance of the staircase before leaving.

On April 6 at approximately 10:24 am, I knew I had to leave my apartment soon if I wanted to make it to work on time. I took one last look at myself in the mirror, wearing a black blouse with black pants and black sandals. As I grabbed my phone, I thought to myself, *I should call Mom*. I decided not to because it would take up too much time and, in turn, I would be late for work. Alright, I know everyone must be thinking now, "DID SHE OR DID SHE NOT MAKE IT TO THE BUS STOP ON TIME?!?!" The answer is yes, I did make it to both the bus stop and work on time! It's all in the small victories, I tell you.

This day was playing out to be the uneventful day I suspected it to be, so much so that I had plenty of time to browse through

Facebook and find other unproductive ways to kill time before it was time for me to head out to class. Now, please don't let this be a reflection of me as a worker. I pride myself on being responsible with completing my work on time and ensuring that I have more productive days than not, but there are simply times when it is OKAY to take it easy. It's called BALANCE, people. Anyway, back to my day.

As I continued to go about my uneventful and unproductive day, I found myself scrolling again through Facebook and noticed that a friend from elementary school had given birth to her first son. He was the cutest little thing, and she seemed so happy. I clicked like on the picture, and a random thought came to mind. *Since this baby was born today, I wonder who is going to die today.* I have had this thought over the years as I have heard people say that for every baby that is born, a person, in turn, dies. My guess is that it serves the purpose of creating a balance between life and death. Perhaps the only way into this world is for someone else to exit and allow your entrance. Never did I ever in a million years think that this precise thought would be a premonition of what was to come.

The day continued, and after calling my friend to wish her a happy birthday, I prepared to leave work and go to school. The class I was heading to was *Adolescent Psychology*, and I had a midterm exam. In an effort to ensure that I arrived at school on time, I asked my co-worker, Al, if he could give me a ride since he was heading in the same direction. It's interesting how life puts all the pieces together at the precise moment without error. As I grabbed my bag to head out the door, I received two incoming calls at the same time: one from my older brother, Raymie, and one from my stepfather, Rodrigo, which was weird. They would usually text me, so if they were both calling me, it was probably because it was something important.

Naturally, I became nervous. My heart started to race, my hands started to sweat, and my breathing felt heavy. I thought to myself, *Whose call do I answer?* I decided to pick up Raymie's call.

Me: Hello?

Raymie: What's going on?

Me: What do you mean, *what's going on?* You called me!

Raymie: Rodrigo just called saying that I have to go home but won't tell me why.

Me: I don't know. He just tried calling me. Let me call him, and I'll call you back.

As the call ended, I started to swallow heavily as I had no idea what my stepfather could be calling me about. The first thing that came to mind was that perhaps my mom was in the hospital again, or perhaps they had gotten into another one of their fights. But if my mom were in the hospital, why would he want my brother to go home? And if perhaps it was another one of their fights, how bad could it have been? But no... this just didn't make sense... mom was doing better now. She no longer was fighting. She was finally different now. I decided to finally quiet my mind and make the call. As my stepfather answered the phone, he had a tone that I had never heard before; it was both a low and serious tone, as though he was trying to hold his emotions inside.

Me: Rodrigo, what's going on? Raymie just called me saying that you asked him to go home.

Rodrigo: Lindsay, you have to come home.

Me: Rodrigo, I can't right now. I have a midterm. What's going on? Is Mom okay?

Rodrigo: Lindsay, you have to come home now.

Me: *screaming and crying* Rodrigo, what the hell is going on? You need to tell me now!

Rodrigo: Lindsay, you have to come home. I can't tell you what's going on over the phone.

After hearing him repeat the same thing over and over, I became filled with anguish. The second I hung up the phone, I felt the umbilical cord get cut off. I tried to reach for it, but it was too late; the connection between my mother and I was cut off. I could no longer feel her. I turned to my co-worker with my eyes filled with tears and said, "I think my mom died."

He walked over and hugged me. He tried to convince me that Mom was probably fine and maybe she was just not feeling well. At this moment, the adrenaline kicked in, and I had to move. I asked Al to drop me off at the Metro North Station so that I could go home. On the drive there, I was trying to hold back my tears and tried to believe Al as he continued to repeat that my mom was probably fine. Life selected Al to be the person with me at that precise moment on purpose, not by coincidence. Al had lost his mother a few years ago and didn't learn the news until he arrived at her home. I can only imagine the flashbacks and emotions that my experience must have brought up for him.

Despite it all, he continued trying to calm me down. The eight to nine-minute drive to the train station felt like an eternity. Time slowed down, and the faster I tried to move, the slower everything around me felt. When we finally arrived at the train station, I changed my mind and decided to take a cab home instead. Al tried to convince me to take the train since a cab from New Rochelle to Manhattan would probably be expensive, but I knew I simply could not wait and had to get home as fast as possible. Luckily, this was during the month of April; I usually saved up money to get my boyfriend at the time a nice birthday gift, so I had a little money in the bank. I ran to the ATM at the station and withdrew $200. I didn't care how much the ride would cost; I just wanted to get home.

As I walked to the cab, my dad called me, and again, the anxiety I was feeling continued to intensify. I answered the phone, and my dad, in a worried tone, asked where I was. Out of impotence and frustration, I started to cry again. I told him I was trying my best to get home as soon as possible. Time just continued to slow down by the minute. He simply said, "Mami, the worst thing you could think of has happened." This was the point at which panic set in. After the divorce, my parents grew to dislike each other. Maybe they even hated each other, so for my dad to call regarding something concerning my mother meant that whatever happened had to be very bad.

The cab finally arrived, and when I got in, the driver saw that I was distressed even as I was trying to hold my composure. As I sat quietly in the backseat, gazing out the window, my phone rang again. I became so angry because people continued to call me but wouldn't tell me what was going on. When I looked at my phone, I saw that it was Raymie calling again. This was the call that nothing or anyone could have prepared me for...

Me: Hello?

Raymie: Lindsay, where are you?

Me: *screaming and crying* I am trying to get home! Why does everyone keep calling me?!?

Raymie: Lindsay *10 second pause* Mom died...

It was at this point that I confirmed what I already knew. The minute I spoke to Rodrigo, the minute I felt the umbilical cord cut off, was when I knew that she was gone. I don't remember much after Raymie told me the news. I don't even remember if I ever hung up the phone. All I remember was my wailing screams with nothing or no one to console me. It felt like a bullet went straight through my heart. I wanted nothing more than to jump out of the car and run home. The driver, who was rightfully alarmed, asked what happened. The only words I was able to put together were, "My mother just died."

I saw the sadness in his eyes through the rearview mirror as he expressed his condolences.

When we finally arrived at my home, I rushed to pay the driver; I don't even know how much I gave him and, quite frankly, didn't care. I just simply wanted to get home. As I got out of the car, I started to run towards the building. The closer I got, the heavier I felt; it was as though I was carrying a bag of bricks around my ankles. I lost all of my energy and felt like I was going to collapse, but still, I continued.

As I walked up the stairs, all I could think was that this day couldn't possibly be real.

This couldn't be true.

This couldn't possibly happen to me.

As I walked down the hallway to the apartment, I knew from that point my life would never be the same. I didn't know what

I would see upon opening the door. I turned the key and walked inside. In the living room, I saw my cousin Francisco, my Aunt Sara, and Rodrigo sitting by the dining table and a police officer by the entrance of the kitchen. I rushed to put my purse down on the couch and then searched for Raymie so that he could explain to me what happened. I found him in my mom's bedroom, and I started to hysterically cry again. Raymie looked at me and gave me a tight hug. As he hugged me, I started to hyperventilate and told him to please get off because I couldn't breathe. My aunt then entered the bedroom and asked if I wanted to see my mom. With tears in my eyes, I looked at her and asked, "What do you mean *see* her?" At this point, the farthest thing in my mind was that my mother was still in the apartment, yet I agreed.

As I walked out of the bedroom towards the living room, I felt intense feelings of anger and frustration. I punched the door, and suddenly, one of my favorite bracelets broke into pieces. This bracelet was gifted to me by a co-worker and represented good luck, so it was befitting that it broke during the most unlucky time of my life.

When I walked into the living room, my aunt pointed to the floor. There, my mother was lying on the floor, with a blanket over her entire body. I couldn't believe that I had not seen her when I first arrived. I couldn't believe it was really her. My mother! I got on my knees and uncovered her, and she looked as though she was sleeping. My mom was typically a deep sleeper, which was mainly a result of the heavy medications she had to take. At times, it was difficult to wake her up, but nonetheless, after enough shaking, she would always wake up. I thought this was one of those times, and no one knew how to wake her. I started to shake her and asked her to please wake up. After several attempts, I became frustrated and spoke louder.

"MOM WAKE UP!"

The police officer who was standing by the kitchen told me to stop moving and touching her.

Feeling defeated, I thought to myself...

My mother, who I had been through hell and back with.

My mother, who fought so hard against her demons.

My mother, who meant everything to me, was now lying lifeless on the apartment floor.

The same apartment that held memories of both happiness and tragedy.

The apartment that was home for some years and a war zone during what felt like a lifetime.

The apartment that I dreaded going to for the simple fact that I never knew what new hell awaited me.

There was nothing I could do at that moment to bring my mother back. All of my previous efforts, battles, and problem-solving skills were gone with the wind because it all came down to this very moment;to this kind of ending.

What seemed to be a new beginning for her, in hindsight, now seemed like a preparation to depart from this world to make things right before she left. During the months leading up to her death, I noticed an airiness about her. She was no longer fighting as much. She smiled more. I actually felt like I could have conversations with her without the fear of upsetting her. We spoke on the phone more often, and I actually wanted to tell her about my days. For the first time in a very long time, I felt like I had a mom. I didn't feel the constant worry I had felt around her for such a long time. Her peace helped me feel at ease.

As I stood up from the floor, I covered Mom with the blanket that she usually used to cover herself when she lay on the couch to watch TV. I walked to the bedroom, feeling numb and confused. I sat on the bed and could hear people continuously come in and out of the apartment. Some of these people, whom I hadn't even seen in many years, were crying and seemingly distraught. To be frank, I think it's pretty shitty to lose contact with a person for many years and then all of a sudden return once the person has passed away. I understand that life happens and people grow apart, but the real tragedy is when people (who were MIA for God knows how long) show up and are suddenly the most concerned, saddest people around. These were the same people who were crying and appeared to be distraught. Give me a fucking break! I couldn't connect to their emotions; I couldn't show myself as vulnerable. In a matter of one to two hours, I went from feeling numb to feeling angry again. I was so angry because all I wanted to do was scream and tell everyone to get out.

All the years that my mother felt alone... All the years that she felt like an outcast... a black sheep. Where were all these people when she needed them? Where were all these people when she needed someone to call and ask how she was doing? Maybe, just maybe, if she had seen and felt people's concern for her, things would have been different for her. I then remembered that my younger brother, Raylin, who lived with my mom at the time, didn't know about my mom's passing. He was at his baseball practice and was expected to arrive home shortly. The last thing we wanted was for Raylin to walk into this kind of scene. I rushed to Raymie and suggested that we wait for Raylin by the entrance of the building.

Before going downstairs, the paramedics arrived to take my

mother's body. The one paramedic asked everyone to clear the living room, but Raymie refused to leave and instead watched as my mother's body was transferred into the black body bag. That was a sight that I am sure forever made an imprint in his mind. Moments later, we went downstairs to intercept Raylin before he could get into the building. As I saw him walking towards the building, my heart accelerated, and I became nervous. Here my brother was, walking to a home that would never be the same.

I quickly told Raymie that I couldn't be the one to tell Raylin the news. Raymie went towards Raylin and took him for a walk. I could already feel Raylin's heart breaking, and it was at that moment that I felt overwhelmed with grief and pain. I would have given everything and anything to have made that moment go away, to have that moment changed. I lived through the dread of knowing that no matter how many times I replayed the entire day in my head, nothing that I did or said would ever change the outcome. My brothers finally returned, and as I watched them walk back toward the building, all I could see was Raylin's tears running down his face. I walked towards him, hugged him, and tried to hold back my tears. I simply felt crushed. He turned to me and asked, "What happened?" All I could say was that I didn't know. Nothing made sense, and I still hoped to open my eyes from this nightmare. Why couldn't I just wake up and see her face again? Touch her one last time. Hear her voice.

The three of us proceeded to go back to the apartment to gather Raylin's belongings because Raymie and I decided it would be best for him not to stay in the apartment. So before walking Raylin inside, I walked ahead of them to let those in my home know to compose themselves and keep it together while Raylin packed his belongings. I've always been protective of both of my brothers, and during this time, I wanted the least amount of turmoil happening around Raylin. I didn't care about being stern or assertive, and to be honest, all I really wanted was for everyone to go away and leave me and my brothers alone. While I appreciated everyone trying to show their support, my mother had already died many times before this final one, and no one but us was there to live through it with her.

As the afternoon turned to night, many of those people who gathered earlier in the day started to leave. My aunts remained, and so did I. I barely felt alive but not quite dead. April 6, 2011, was by far the longest day of my life, and I felt as though it was never going to come to an end. At some point, they went to bed, but I decided to stay in the living room with the TV on for the background noise. I stared at the couch that my mom usually laid on and continued to replay all of the possible scenarios of the moments leading up to her death. But still, nothing made sense. While playing the scenarios in my head, I also wished and prayed that I would hear the front door open and see my mom walking in. One of my dogs, Suzie, my mom's favorite, lay by the door for weeks, waiting for the one person who would never come back. Suzie and I remained with the false hope that someday Mom would return. This could not be life. This could not be real.

Eventually, after a few hours, I went into the shower, and that's where I crumbled. With my silent cries, I sat under the water and felt every tear, heartbreak, and overwhelming pain that consumed my existence. Still, it was not enough to kill me. I've felt alone for a long time, but this was a different type of loneliness, one that I had not felt before. This loneliness was accompanied by the reality that the life before April 6, 2011, would never come back no matter how hard I tried. Nothing compared to this kind of pain. I have been able to overcome a lot of things in this life, no matter how hard, painful, or sour the experience. But the death of my creator, my maker, my half, my everything was something that I could not, would not, overcome. As I went to bed, I lay there staring at the blanket that was used to cover my mother's body. As the hours passed, I spent the night staring and listening to the cries of my aunts, who would awaken every so often.

Out of all the deaths that I lived through, this, by far, was the worst one. I was sure that I wouldn't survive it. Not because I couldn't but because I didn't want to. A life without my mom was not a life but rather a death sentence. Ironically, that's the same sentiment I felt with her for several years. I felt that living with her was a death sentence that I didn't sign up for; none of us did.

The sunrise finally came, and everyone went into the living room to wait for my grandmother to arrive from the Dominican Republic. As we sat there in silence, my aunts started to cry again. At one point, one of them turned to me and said, "I wish I had your strength. Look how, at the age of 20, you're able to hold it together while I am an older woman and can't seem to keep my composure."

To respond to my aunt would have required energy that I didn't have. As I stared at her, inside was a shattered soul; inside, I was dead. Yet the lack of tears or lack of expressed emotions was translated into strength. A strength that I had lost a long time ago. What my aunt and other people didn't realize was that I was running on autopilot. I no longer belonged to me. This wasn't my existence. I checked out. April 6, 2011. The date that will forever haunt me in my waking and sleeping life.

Chapter 2

PICTURE PERFECT LINDSAY

Has there ever been a time in which you felt that being yourself wasn't enough? Have you ever been so far from yourself that when you looked in the mirror, you couldn't recognize the person staring back at you? There was once upon a time when I felt like me. When I felt that I was happy...until I wasn't anymore.

I can't remember exactly when the shift happened, but I know that it was around the time that my mother's medical issues and ongoing surgeries started. There was something about the way I saw my mother agonize in pain that told me that I could not I should not be happy during this time. She would frequently have trouble sleeping at night because of her back pain, and therefore, most of her sleeping happened during the day. My dad would tell my brothers and me that we had to keep quiet to avoid waking her up when we were home. We minimized the noise, and we also stopped seeing Mom. When she would wake up, it would be to either shower or eat, as her pain medications couldn't be taken on an empty stomach. Little by little, I saw her fading, and little by little, I started to fade as well.

As a kid, I loved spending time with my mom, but due to her medical issues, our time together was minimal. It all started with her chronic back pains, which, over time, got worse. And with every suggested surgery, it seemed as though she fell deeper into the hole and came out with more pain than before. My mom had a total of seven spinal surgeries and one brain surgery. She wanted to be free from her debilitating pain. She agreed to every surgery and to every newly prescribed medication. She just wanted to be out of pain.

Most of her surgeries happened when my brothers and I were kids. Every time she would return home after a surgery, I didn't know what to think or say about all that was happening, so I just shrugged it off and did what I was told: be quiet so as not to disturb her rest. A part of me had some hope that one day, my mom would take the right medication or have a successful surgery that would alleviate all of her issues, but unfortunately, as time went by, the pain only intensified, and the mom we knew was no longer there. She tried her best to be present, but the pain she experienced consumed her waking hours, so it was difficult for her to focus on anything else. Looking back on it now, I realize that the pain, ongoing surgeries, and never-ending medication list all came as thieves in the night. Her pain robbed me and my brothers from truly seeing her, as all we were faced with was the pain she endured from the continuous cycle of surgeries and medications.

Life growing up in my household would be considered relatively normal. My mom worked at a hospital before Raylin was born. After he arrived, she became a stay-at-home mom while my dad worked. My mom and grandmother would alternate taking my brothers and me to school as well as picking us up. I remember back in kindergarten, something happened at school that had me praying and wishing that Mom wouldn't pick me up. I went to a Catholic school and became friends with this boy who was considered a "troublemaker." He was often punished for not listening or doing something he wasn't supposed to do.

We had assigned seating, and he sat at a table next to mine. During nap time, my friend and I did the opposite of napping. (BOY, WHAT I WOULD GIVE TO HAVE NAP TIME TODAY!). As my friend and I were NOT napping, we started to horseplay and hit each other playfully. Nap time was finally coming to an end. I was so excited because the class was going to watch the movie *Toy Story* afterward. Little did I know that the teacher had other plans for my friend and me. To my surprise, our teacher saw us horsing around, and right when the movie was getting ready to begin, she called both of us over to her desk.

"What were you doing during nap time?" she asked. I was too young to realize that she already knew the answer to that question. Not wanting to get in trouble, I lied and said I was napping. Unfortunately, my friend gave in under pressure and confessed that we were messing around. I became filled with anxiety and fear as I was not used to getting in trouble over anything. I normally followed the rules and did what I was told, yet here I was at the age of five, about to be punished for playing instead of napping and then lying about it! So I did what I think any other child would do in this situation: I lied. AGAIN.

"It's all his fault!" I yelled. "He hit me first, so I hit him back!" This was not completely false, the same way it wasn't completely true! I was definitely an active participant, and I was having fun, but the thought of getting in trouble was something that I could not mentally cope with. It was too bad that the lie didn't get me out of trouble because the teacher decided to take away movie time, and we had to face the wall until the movie was over. As I walked up to the wall, I felt like my world had collapsed. I was five years old and felt that, for the first time, I didn't do things correctly or perfectly. I regretted ever having played with my friend during naptime. I regretted that entire afternoon. I resented my friend because he came up with this game in the first place. I felt like a failure. I heard my friends laughing while watching the movie. The same movie that I wanted to watch but couldn't because I was busy playing silly games with a troublemaker. I should've known better!

As the movie ended and my teacher turned the lights back on, she told my friend and me to start getting ready for dismissal. I sighed in relief because my punishment was finally over... or so I thought! As I began putting on my jacket, my teacher approached me.

"Who's picking you up this afternoon?" she asked.

"I don't know," I truthfully responded.

"Well, whoever it is, I need to speak with them!"

At this moment, I started having cold sweats, and I could feel my breathing getting heavier and heavier. I felt an intense feeling in the pit of my stomach. I was worried that I'd see my mother coming through the classroom door instead of my grandmother, so I did the only thing I could do at that moment: I prayed.

My parents and my teachers always taught me that whenever you are in need, all you have to do is pray and ask God to help you. So, I decided to put my learning to practice. Even to this day, I pray with such intensity and angst when I am in a difficult situation, hoping that a miracle will happen and things will work out.

Funny enough, as I was writing this chapter, my laptop decided to shut down. As soon as I restarted it and tried to open up my draft for the chapter, which, by the way, was nearly finished, it would not open. My chapter displayed an error message stating that the document was a corrupt file and, therefore, couldn't open. At this moment, I, like the 5-year-old me, started sweating cold and felt my breathing getting heavier. I tried 101 different suggestions I researched online, yet the error message was still the same. Thoughts were racing, but nothing was working. I had dedicated several hours to this chapter, which I was specifically proud of because I got to explore the childhood version of me. But it seemed that the scared Lindsay, who was present at five years old, was still very much present at the age of 29. I started to regret not having anticipated that my laptop would crash.

I became angry with myself. Why? Why couldn't I figure this out? Here was the 29-year-old Lindsay returning to the 5-year-old, who thought she had to be perfect. The Lindsay that couldn't make a mistake. The Lindsay that should've known better. One would think that 24 years later, things would change. But somehow and in some way, life has a way of bringing us back to our childhood versions of ourselves. I knew I would eventually have to rewrite the chapter, but how? I had already thoroughly expressed my thoughts the first time around. Would I be able to do the same the second time around? After a migraine from stress set in, I became upset that I couldn't get upset the way people normally do. Why couldn't I scream, cry, or roll on the ground? At least then, the anger would be able to leave my system. Instead, I internalized my anger and frustration and ended up with a good ol' raging migraine that felt like the size of Texas. I decided to call it a night and resorted to a prayer of angst and desperation before going to sleep. I prayed for a miracle like I did at five years old.

The morning came, and the reality remained the same. I felt defeated. The frustration had subsided, but I was not motivated to restart this chapter. How would I phrase things in the same manner as I did the first time? At some point, I was able to retrieve some of the content from the chapter. I felt elated. I felt relieved. While it wasn't the complete chapter, it was still enough to be able to continue. This showed me that while, yes, it was frustrating to face my fear of losing my work, it still wasn't the end of the world, even though it may have felt like it.

As I calmed myself and filled myself with gratitude, I spoke to the five-year-old Lindsay and told her that things would always be okay no matter how difficult life would get. And even when they aren't okay right away, nothing that I do or have done warrants negative self-talk or self-blame for making mistakes. Am I also not human? Even now, I still forget that small detail. I am perfectly imperfect, and that is okay.

During my prayer at school that memorable day, I asked God to send my grandmother as I knew that she would be much more understanding of the situation and I could sweet talk her much easier. If God couldn't send my grandmother, then I asked that He wipe both my mom's and grandmother's memory clean, and they'd forget to pick me up for the day. Either scenario would've been fine by me! For some reason, I felt like I was a huge disappointment, and I had no one else to blame except myself (and the troublemaker, of course!). I don't even know why I had this intense level of anxiety and fear because, during this time, I don't remember my mom having done anything up to that point that would have indicated that she would've disowned me after this incident. But still, the fear and angst persisted.

After waiting for what felt like an eternity, finally, my person arrived to pick me up. As I stood up from my table and put on my backpack, I watched the door open, only to see my mother in the flesh! My face dropped, and I wondered why God had not answered my prayers. Having to take matters into my own hands, I bolted like lightning to my mom and started pushing her out of the classroom, telling her we had to leave immediately. She looked confused and asked me what was wrong. I looked at her and said, "Mom, please! We have to go!" as my little arms tried to push her through the door. As she was finally getting ready to take me home, my teacher yelled from across the classroom and told my mom to wait as she wanted to talk to her. If there was a moment that I wanted to die or have the earth swallow me, it was at this exact moment. I started to cry and told my mom not to believe anything that my teacher said about me.

I can't imagine a child at the age of five feeling this kind of terror. My teacher walked over to my mom and told her what had happened during naptime. As she spoke, I looked down and hated her for doing this to me. She had already punished me. She had already taken my right to movie time. Wasn't this enough?! Now, I had to face my mom and her disappointment.

After my teacher got done tattling, my mom told her that she would talk to me once we got home. I knew that "I will talk to her at home" probably meant "I am going to punish her so that she will learn to not behave this way." My heart continued to sink, and I knew that my life was doomed. I left school hating my teacher, hating my friend, and hating myself. Why did this day have to happen?

As we walked home, my mom held my hand, and I was completely silent. I wasn't crying. I wasn't speaking. In fact, I tried not to breathe loudly in order not to make noise. I didn't know what awaited me at home, but I was sure it wasn't good. When we got home, I sat in the living room and waited for the sentencing of my punishment. My mom put her purse down and very calmly asked me to tell her what happened at school. I stuck to my story and explained to her that during nap time, my friend hit me, so I hit him back. As my eyes filled with tears, my mom looked at me and said, "Lindsay, it's okay. I am not mad. Next time, when someone hits you, make sure to hit them harder!" Sweet baby! This was music to my ears! My tears quickly dried up, and my angst, fear, and worry all dissipated while I looked at my mother with a smile of relief.

"So I'm not in trouble?"

"No," she responded. "You didn't hit first."

In my family, we grew up with the culture of "if someone hits you, then you hit them back" as a means to make sure that people didn't take advantage of us or bully us. I looked up and quietly thanked God because He didn't answer my prayers the way that I had asked Him to, but He definitely provided me with an even better outcome. I felt relieved. I felt joy. All the tension slipped away from my little body, and then I ran off to my room to play with my brothers. I felt like the happiest kid at that time because my mom showed me mercy.

Looking back on this time makes me wonder what was going on with me internally that made me unable to fathom the thought of ever getting into trouble or doing things the wrong way. Why, as a five-year-old, could I not make a mistake? Why, at the age of five, did I already take life too seriously? Why did I think that I needed to be perfect? To my recollection, my mom had never done anything to make me feel this way, yet I did. And even now, at the age of 29, I still ask myself these questions.

In the past, I've reflected on the expectations and standards that I've set for myself, and to be honest, it makes me sad because I haven't always allowed myself to be flexible or fallible. I've been downright rigid. While I have come a long way sometimes, I still revert to my old ways. Take exercise, for example. Although I enjoy exercising, movements that require the body to be relaxed are usually difficult for me because I don't know how to be at ease. I am always worried about making a mistake and getting hit with some sort of exercise equipment or toppling over somewhere if I lose my balance. But what would be the worst that could happen if my fears actually came true? Say, if I did get hit with a piece of equipment or topple over, there's a chance that I'd be hurt, but would I die and fall into the pits of hell? Probably not. Nonetheless, this is how I have conditioned my mind and body to respond to life in general, whether there is a threat or not.

Now, back to kindergarten, yet again! My experience as a five-year-old led me to want to avoid these feelings of angst, fear, and regret. I saw myself becoming what others needed me to be. In fact, I couldn't process the thought of breaking the rules or misbehaving. This wasn't me. I knew that while other kids my age got into trouble, I couldn't be like them. There was something internally that was stopping me from being like them. I had to be the one who understood the rules and understood right from wrong. I needed to make sure that I kept myself and those around me in check.

As I got older, this feeling of having to be perfect increased. In school, I was considered the "teacher's pet" in almost every grade. The teachers trusted me and would send me to make copies for them or pick up supplies from the principal's office. I felt good about this. I felt like I was doing things the right way because I followed the rules, paid attention in class, was nice to the teachers, and didn't disrupt the class. I pleased my teachers. I pleased my parents. And I didn't have to worry about anyone saying anything negative about me. I remember one time in the fourth grade, my teacher became frustrated with the class and assigned everyone lines to write. Everyone except me. I was looked upon as the perfect student, and oftentimes, the teacher would use me as an example. "Everyone," she would say, "take a look at Lindsay. You should model her behavior. She listens and follows the rules!" Every time the teacher praised my angelic behavior amongst the other 4th-grade rioters, my friends would look at me angrily. After a while, though, they realized that I simply didn't get into trouble.

Back at home, my mother's health continued to decline, which required all of us to step up. My mom started to experience intense back pain that would sometimes leave her feeling paralyzed, so my grandma, who is like a second mom to me, would cook, clean, and take my brothers and me to school when my mom wasn't able to. On the other hand, my dad spent a lot of time working, trying to provide for the family. He also helped out in the home when he could. Given all that was going on, I knew that the expectation of me behaving and following the rules was that much greater. My family already had enough going on, and I didn't want them to worry about me. So, I learned to become self-sufficient and did many things, such as showering, brushing my teeth, and doing my homework without being prompted by an adult. I tried my best not to add anything to my family's plate, which was already too full.

As the years passed, my mom's health continued to be the center of my family's focus. When I got old enough, I became her little nurse and helped her take her medication. I took this job very seriously, and despite being unable to read all the medications, I made sure that I was very careful not to make a mistake. My mom would often point to the medication bottle that she needed at any point, but to eliminate the possibility of me making a mistake, I would bring the medicine close to her eyes to confirm. I couldn't make a mistake because I didn't want to be the reason that something bad happened to her.

Looking back, I think that caring for my mom in that way contributed to the continued pressure of me being "perfect" but also my internal feeling of always wanting to help others no matter how big or small the aid needed. I remember whenever my brothers would come home hurt or my friends might have fallen on the playground, I was always the first to try to help and fill a need. My family appeared to have noticed this innate yearning to help because my cousins would call me a "people pleaser" because anytime I was asked what I wanted to do, I would respond with "Whatever you want to do." I didn't appreciate the name-calling, but, to be honest, I felt good when I had things to do and when I was useful to others.

Fast forward to the eighth grade, my last year of middle school. My mother had remarried by this time to my stepfather and had gone to Mexico with him for some time to have a church wedding and spend time with his family. During this time, my grandmother was our sole caretaker because my dad was in the Dominican Republic, running away from my mom. After being incarcerated

3 times, he wanted to be as far away from her as possible so that she couldn't harm him anymore (don't worry; you'll read more about this over the next few chapters).

I remember one week before my eighth-grade graduation, I spoke to my mom over the phone and asked her if she would come back home for my graduation. She paused and said, "Yes." I felt happy at that moment because even though I wouldn't have both my parents present, at least I would have my mom. The days went by, and still no sign that my mom would be coming back any time soon. I soon realized that she probably would not be present at my graduation. The day before the ceremony, my classmates and I rehearsed and made the final preparations. My school had a tradition for the eighth graders, where each student would give one rose to a parent, usually the mom, as a symbol of gratitude for supporting them through their academic careers. My teacher went around the classroom asking each student which parent they planned to give the rose to. When it was my turn to speak, I didn't know what to say. I put my head down on my desk, in between my arms, and started to cry. I cried because I knew that neither one of my parents would be there. I cried because I felt like I wasn't worth them being there. I cried because a part of me felt like I had done something to deserve this. I cried because even though I was an honor student, it still seemed to not be enough.

My teacher and friends tried to console me and suggested that I give the rose to my grandmother, who would be present that day. I said nothing about this, but in my heart, I knew that I didn't want to give the rose to anyone else who wasn't my parents. I quickly wiped my tears and resorted to my typical phrase, "I'm fine. It's fine." I urged the next student to report to whom they would give their rose to take the attention away from myself.

My graduation came, and the naïve part of me still hoped my mom would surprise me by showing up. Every time the doors to the church opened, I turned around to see if it was her. After a while, the doors stopped opening. My mother never showed up. My grandmother, brothers, and aunt attended the ceremony. I was grateful to see them there, but I couldn't help but feel numb to the experience. At that point, I felt like all my efforts were for nothing. I clearly had not worked hard enough. Otherwise, my parents my mom would have been there. The time came to give out the roses, and as I picked mine up, I walked to my grandmother with a knot in my throat. I gave her the rose and thanked her for taking care of my brothers and me. As I hugged her, I wanted to cry because I was in pain. But instead, I held it inside and walked back to my seat. The ceremony ended, and I took pictures with my friends. I felt relieved that it was over. Now, I could go back home and stop pretending to be happy when I wasn't. It was exhausting, and I needed a break. Little did I know that I would continue to feel this exhaustion of pretending to be something other than me. To the world, I was happy. To myself, I was in pain. I was depressed. I was anxious. And still, I felt like it was my fault.

As the years went by, I continued to try my hardest to give it my all, hoping that I would someday feel as though I was finally enough. I knew I had to do something if I wanted a different outcome. I continuously ran into the same rabbit hole. I worked myself to the ground only to look around me and see no one. I felt like I didn't matter. Relationship after relationship, I felt the same sense of worthlessness that I felt at home. I was the girlfriend who was spontaneous. I was the girlfriend who liked to surprise her boyfriend with things that would make him happy. I was the girlfriend who put his needs in front of my own. Besides, wasn't it my job to make others happy?

I felt connected in every relationship. I even asked myself a few times if he could be the one. Could he be the one to finally help me feel whole? Could he be the one to give me the happiness that I, myself, couldn't find? Could he be the one to fill the void? Could he be the one to make me feel as though I was enough? Every single time, the answer was no. No, he wasn't the one. Even though I already saw the red flags pointing at the fact that he or any of them wasn't the one, I still persisted and tolerated. I tolerated more than I should have with the hopes that things would get better. Things never got better, and these were the lies I told myself in order to keep doing, keep fighting, and keep the relationship alive. I noticed that after several of my relationships, I felt the same with each one of them. I felt as though I was single-handedly carrying the weight of the relationship. I felt that I was the one trying to make the relationship work. I felt that while I was with someone, I was still alone.

I later came to realize that in my boyfriends, I was looking for all the things I didn't have at home. I was looking for a sense of belonging. I was looking to be loved. I was exhausted and soon gave up hope that I would ever find anyone who would want to be with me. Again, I felt worthless. I felt like perhaps I didn't try enough. Perhaps I left too soon. Perhaps I wasn't patient enough. With my mom, I learned to tolerate. With my mom, I learned to stick through the good, the bad, and the in-between. But still, the outcome remained the same. I was alone. It wasn't long before I became hopeless. I figured that happiness and love were simply not in the cards for me. I tried tirelessly, yet I seemed to fail every single time. By this time, I was so far away from myself that the only times I truly looked in the mirror were in the mornings and evenings when I brushed my teeth by the bathroom sink. I looked into my eyes and saw nothing. By this time, I had been so far away from who I was that I could no longer see life in my face, in my eyes.

I no longer wanted to feel disappointed or run into the same rabbit hole that I was all too familiar with. I became more and more depressed, and very few noticed it because, on the outside, I seemed fine. I went to school. I worked during my high school years. I had friends. I still laughed. So, what could be wrong with me? Everything!

I learned how to operate on autopilot. True to form, I continued to excel academically. I continued to work and tend to my responsibilities, but inside, I felt dead. My mother's death was the tip of the iceberg, and I felt that after that, there was nothing else to look forward to. There was nothing to look forward to, and at the same time, I continued to tend to my responsibilities. For a long time, I existed through the days as though I was waiting for my own time to come when I would no longer be here and feel this immense amount of pain and sadness. Yet, no one saw this. I was able to put on a good show for people so that my mask of happiness and normalcy would be the way people saw me.

I thought I was a great actress until one day, during the drive back home, my cousin looked at me and asked if I was okay. Without even thinking of the question, I automatically responded, "I'm fine." He looked at me again and told me that he didn't think I was fine. He told me that he could see through me and the person I was trying to present versus the person I actually was. He told me that he saw that I was still tending to my responsibilities and working hard, but for some reason, I wasn't connected to any of it. He looked at me and told me that it was as though I was existing and not living. I started to cry. For the first time in a long time, someone saw me without my mask on. For the first time in a long time, someone saw my pain and agony and cared enough to ask about it. It was during this time that I knew that my mask had become so heavy that I could no longer bear it. I felt hopeless, defeated, depressed, lost, disconnected, and with no direction. I was exhausted from trying. I was exhausted from living. I didn't know how or what to change to avoid feeling this way.

Because I had no sense of direction and had already tried so hard for years to be something other than unhappy, I accepted once again that happiness and love were simply not in my future. In December 2016, I made the decision that I wanted out. I was exhausted from being this exhausted, and if there was something that I could do, it was to take myself out of my own agony, my own existence. I didn't want to continue settling to just exist. I used to want to live, but not anymore. I wanted to be with my mom. The person for whom I tried to be enough. In December 2016, I ended my seven-year relationship with my boyfriend at the time. This was a relationship that, while it served a great purpose in my life, was also something that I was holding onto for fear of being alone and not being wanted by anyone else. The end of this relationship felt like a relief because this relationship had been ending for a long time until I finally decided to cut the cord. While I felt relieved then, I also felt that it put my plan in place to not be here anymore. I thought of the different ways I could do it. *Would it be through an overdose?* No, I ran the risk of surviving and just having really bad stomach pains. *Would I slit my wrists?* No, this seemed too gruesome. I couldn't do this to myself. *Would I hang myself?* No, I didn't want to traumatize my aunt, who I was living with at the time. *How could I do it?*

After nights of thinking long and hard about this, something inside me told me to try for the last time. Try to give it my all for the last time, with the hopes that things would change. That things would get better. And then, if this last time failed, I would end it finally. In January 2017, I got myself into therapy, and so my journey to healing and self-discovery began. I felt like someone finally heard my pain. Several times, my therapist had to validate the intensity of my experiences, especially during the times that I tried to minimize them. That is the thing about being used to being in survival mode; you don't realize you are simply surviving and getting by until someone on the other side points it out.

During my first year in therapy, I felt like I had someone to share my pain with. I had someone who didn't judge me or tell me I was doing things wrong. In fact, I had someone who empathized and expressed her sorrow for me. She expressed sorrow for me having to have experienced the pain that I did. She told me during one session that the first time she looked into my eyes, she saw what looked like a zombie; someone who was simply existing. Week after week, I gave a home to my pain. Week after week, I learned that my life wasn't my fault and that I was perfectly imperfect. Week after week, I still felt my depression, loneliness, and anxiety, but now I felt less hopeless.

She soon encouraged me to start running, as I had mentioned that I always wanted to be like the people who ran no matter the weather. When she suggested that I start running, I thought I wouldn't be able to since I was a solid 200 pounds at the height of 5'3 and didn't have one athletic bone in my body. She insisted enough times that I decided to start, and it was exactly as challenging as I thought it would be. Except that no matter how challenging it got, I persisted and finished the set number of miles that I had aimed to complete. As I continued to train, my therapist invited me to a local race in which she and her family were participating. I decided to join, and 700 meters from the finish line, I fell and sprained my ankle.

I would have never imagined that I would ever be participating in a race. Even though I didn't finish the race because of my sprain, exactly one month later, I was back for the last race of the season. I was not exactly cleared to run during this time, but I felt good and felt like I had to vindicate myself and finish the race I had started. The race came, and I saw several runners who had previously helped me during my fall. They were all so encouraging and loving. I felt connected. I felt that I was a part of their community. I finished the race, and the rest has been history. Three years later, I have run dozens of races, including two NYC Marathons. I also forgot to mention that I went from 200 pounds to now 130 pounds, a total of 70 pounds lost. The 70 pounds were not easy to lose, but with every pound, I proved to myself that I was fighting. That I was pushing forward. While I didn't know the destination, I was trying to give myself a fighting chance. I was trying to find myself again.

These experiences have helped me reflect and learn so many things about myself that I don't think I would have known otherwise. These experiences, which felt like failures, actually forced me to look within myself and find the things that I was searching for in others. These experiences helped me look within myself and see the different parts of myself that I never knew existed before. These experiences taught me that I can't expect others to fill the void that only I can fill. These experiences taught me that I am imperfectly perfect the way I am, with flaws and all. These experiences have taught me that I am enough. That I am a fighter. And that I have been courageous enough to walk through the dark, to walk through the fire, and even during my darkest hours, I still kept going. I even have a tattoo on my left wrist with the words "keep going" as a permanent and gentle reminder to not give up no matter how difficult things get. While I can't say today that I have learned completely how to love myself, I can at least say that I am on that journey. I am also still in the process of finding Lindsay. I know that when I find her, it will be beautiful.

I will end with a note to the five-year-old Lindsay, who was scared shitless to make a mistake.

Lindsay,

You are beautiful. You are kind. You are enough. I know right now you feel as though you can't be like other kids because you have to be perfect. But I am here to tell you that you are imperfectly perfect the way you are. Lindsay, life is going to get hard. Life is going to get dark. There will be times you will feel like it is your fault because somewhere along the lines, you learned that you were responsible for the way others treated you. Lindsay, you were born to live. You will feel lost. You will start to lose bits and pieces of yourself. You will start to leave behind the Lindsay that once was. Lindsay, I am sorry for having to leave you. I am sorry that I had to lock you away in order to be the person that I needed to be to survive. Lindsay, I promise you that as soon as I can, I will come back for you, and you will be safe again. Lindsay, I love you, and the world can't wait to meet the woman you are today, tomorrow, and forever.

Chapter 3:

MY MOTHER'S KEEPER

For years, I looked up to my mom as my role model. I saw her as someone who could do no wrong. I looked to her for guidance, and I seldom questioned her actions and assumed that everything she did and said was right. Isn't that how most kids look at their parents? For some reason, we tend to have the preconceived notion that our parents have it all figured out and have all the answers. It's not until we grow up and face the real world that we realize that adults are simply trying to do their best and that we are far from having life "figured out."

As a kid, I thought that my parents had all of the connections in the world; they had the address for God and Santa Claus, and they also had a relationship with a nosey little bird that would tell them all of the bad things my brothers and I would do. Every time my parents lectured me about something that I did wrong, their response would start with, "A little birdie told me…" I swore that if I ever found this bird, I would smack it and ask why it insisted on getting me in trouble. Lucky for the bird, I never found him or her.

I was approximately seven years old when my mom started to have ongoing spinal surgeries. During one of my mother's surgeries, I asked my dad when I could see my mom again. He looked at me with sad eyes and told me, "Soon. Soon she will be back home." I could see my father's pain through his glazed eyes. He tried to be strong and not show us that he was worried or that he was feeling distressed. But inside, I knew there was something different. I told him I wanted her to know I missed her and wanted her to feel better. He told me that I couldn't visit her but that I could write a letter to God asking Him to heal her so that she wouldn't have to go back to the hospital. He explained that he would then mail the letter to God so that He could read it directly.

I sat down and wrote two full pages, asking God to please heal my mom. I pleaded with God. I bargained with God. I even wrote a good character reference letter for my mom in case he had any concerns about her. I promised God that I would always be good if He would simply heal her and allow her to be her again. I thought this detailed, well-thought-out letter would do the trick. But after several more surgeries, I began to wonder if something might have happened with the post office that did not allow for God to receive the letter. I knew my dad should have sent it through certified mail!

After every surgery came a certain level of hopelessness. I saw it in both my dad's and mom's faces, along with pain, both physical and mental. The woman I saw as my role model now spent her days lying on a bed, sedated by pain medications. Unfortunately, my parents didn't talk much to us about the situation, which brought me a sadness that I hadn't experienced before. In an effort to help, I became quieter. I became invisible. I no longer saw myself because all I could see was my mother's pain. Even at this tender age, I didn't yearn for the common things that kids my age liked and wanted. I simply told myself to not make noise or disturb my parents. I didn't complain about anything because my needs were secondary to everything that was happening with my mom. Instead, I spent my time looking for ways to be more independent so as to not worry or stress my parents more than they already were. I stopped by her room frequently to check in on her and to see if she needed anything. Her needs began to increase, and so did my duties as her "nurse." I went from simply handling her medications to being at her beck and call. I didn't have any particular feelings towards this at the time, though now, looking back at it, a huge part of me believes that around this time was when I first learned to numb myself. I learned to detach myself from any emotional response because to have an emotional response would distract me from my focus: my mom. It would require me to experience intense emotions that I was not prepared to face, which would make me lose control. To experience emotion would not have paired well with the put-together persona that I showed the world. I could not fall apart because what good would I be to my mother?

After my parents' divorce, which you will read about in more detail in later chapters, my sense of responsibility to take care of my mom only intensified. It was as though my mom and I had reversed roles. I found myself worrying about her and making sure that things were done for her around the house, and I accompanied her to medical appointments when she needed me to. I was concerned for her, as a parent would worry for their child. There were times when she asked for my opinion or advice regarding certain situations. Our relationship changed from me looking up to her for guidance to now having her look to me for that same guidance. What did I know about life? Not much! But I sure as hell made sure to figure it out each step of the way.

People today still ask me how I am able to solve what they consider to be "huge problems" in a matter of minutes. My brain just became conditioned to constantly work and process information to help me come up with the best possible set of solutions for most day-to-day issues. Over time, I became more creative and innovative in my thinking, but it also started to wear on me and drain the few ounces of energy I had left. There were times when I couldn't even look at myself in the mirror or even say anything out loud because I felt depleted from overworking my mind and constantly feeling the pressure to DO; I couldn't just sit down and be. I couldn't be present and in the moment because I had to plan and figure things out.

Attending appointments with my mom kept me in the loop about what was going on with her physically and allowed me to advocate for her when she wouldn't do it herself. There were times in which she would downplay the symptoms that she was experiencing, and I was able to interject and elaborate on her symptoms in their entirety based on my observations at home.

Being my mom's advocate was not an easy transition for me, as I was a timid, soft-spoken kid who followed the rules and didn't normally talk back to adults. There came a time when I realized that the world didn't see my mom as I saw her. For some reason, she was dismissed and invalidated by those on the outside. It was as though she carried the stigma of being the black sheep, but I couldn't understand why at that point. All I knew was that I didn't like how the world treated her, so "Lindsay the Pitbull" was born.

At least, that was one of the nicknames, among others, that I have received from family and friends. I didn't want to become this person, but I didn't have any other choice. It was either that or let people mistreat and disrespect my mom. And I couldn't let the latter happen.

Anytime I witnessed either a medical professional or a random person trying to mistreat her by speaking to her condescendingly or disrespectfully, I jumped to her defense. I felt like it was my job to help my mom feel safe. I started to see the world as being cruel and not understanding of all the struggles that she was experiencing at the time. They were mean to her, so I became even meaner. The more defensive of my mom I became, the colder inside I felt. That little timid, people-pleasing, scared Lindsay was being pushed deeper and deeper inside the cave. I couldn't be scared even when I was. I had to be tough because if not me, then who would keep my mom safe? I saw her as someone who needed to be protected from the world and eventually realized that she would also need to be protected from herself.

I have to say that my mother became and represented a lot of different things for me. There were times when my mother was my best friend, and there were other times when it felt like she was my enemy. There were times she was loving, and there were other times when she was hateful. Regardless of the experience good, bad, neutral, or traumatizing I could always see the real her deep down inside. Even during the times that she was not her "normal" self, I still knew she was in there somewhere. She just had the tendency to get lost inside of herself and needed some help finding her way back again.

Has it ever happened to you where someone close to you did or said something hurtful, but for some reason, you were able to forgive them and continue loving them because you knew deep down they were either scared or struggling with their own demons? Well, my mom had many of those demons. Sometimes, she was driven by them; other times, she fought like hell to resist and push them away. Through each encounter, I always saw her. I think my mom's best way to fight her internal demons was to try to escape the only way she knew how: death.

Death seemed like a nirvana that would take her out of her emotional and physical pain. Death seemed like the release that she had been searching for most of her life. It seemed as though she had become hopeless of ever being able to step out of her world of pain. Death represented the unknown. But it also represented the end of everything, including her pain. My mom never truly talked about it, but the few times she did, she expressed the extreme loneliness that she felt inside. She felt that no matter how many people were around her, she always felt alone and disconnected.

Shortly after my parents' divorce, my mom lost her rock and her support system, which was my dad. She had to face life alone with us and didn't know how to simultaneously battle her demons. She tried to release herself from the pain through suicide attempts, which you will read about more in the chapters ahead. Each time that she slit her wrist and tried to overdose on medication, I felt like I was in a whirlwind and didn't know how to get out. During the times that she tried to overdose on her medication, I would call the ambulance against her will, and she would then be admitted into the psychiatric unit.

My first time visiting her at the psychiatric unit was horrible. This was my first experience with entering a place that had such an intense level of security. I had to go through several locked doors to simply see my mom. The visiting hours were limited, and we had no privacy. I remember even being patted down to ensure that I wasn't bringing her anything from the outside. I wasn't even able to bring her food. As I sat with her in the common area, I felt a knot in my throat as I looked at her in such a frazzled state. She looked scared, and I felt guilty about calling the ambulance. I was conflicted because I didn't want my mom to die from an overdose, but I also didn't want her to be locked inside a psychiatric unit where she had no rights. She was seen as a walking disease instead of a human. She had been previously diagnosed with bipolar disorder, then schizophrenia, and then borderline personality disorder. These varied diagnoses, in my mind, proved that the doctors didn't *see* her; they simply saw her as being defective.

As I sat with her, I tried to make small talk in an effort to distract her from the hell that she was in. I asked her how she was feeling, and she told me that she was feeling better. I looked into her eyes and felt the enormous pain that she felt inside. She didn't have to say the words; in my heart, I knew she was living inside her own hell.

I looked around and saw that all of the patients were spread out at different tables. Some were watching TV. Others were playing board games, and some were pacing back and forth, talking to themselves. The energy in the common area was tense, and the nurses stood like guards along with the actual security. No one was smiling. People just seemed to be in a trance. I felt like I was in the twilight zone, and for some reason, my mom was here. She didn't *act* like them or *look* like them, but here she was.

My mom looked thinner, and she confessed that since she didn't like the food, she hadn't eaten much, so I went up to one of the nurses and asked if I could at least bring her some fruit to eat. She looked at me and referred me to the Visitor Rules, which indicated that visitors were not permitted to bring in anything for the patients. The nurse explained that it was related to safety issues. I looked at her and explained that my mom wasn't eating. The nurse responded by saying that my mom was making the choice to not eat. I remember being filled with rage. I wanted to tackle this nurse to the ground, but I remained composed. I felt the rage in my bloodstream, but I knew the consequences that would arise as a result of my acting out. Hell, I would have probably been locked inside the unit myself or been arrested if I had acted on my impulse. I understood the rules, but I also understood that as a professional, people have the choice of being human first or professional first. She didn't care that my mother was losing weight because she wasn't eating. There was nothing in her facial expression that signaled compassion. There was just a bleak stare.

In an effort to maintain my visiting rights, I walked back to my mom and told her that I tried to convince the nurse to allow me to bring her food, but she didn't budge. My mom smiled at me and told me that it was okay. But the truth was that it was not okay for me. I felt as though it was my fault that my mom was there in the first place, and now, she was suffering the consequences. *Why the hell did I have to call the ambulance? Why couldn't I have just tried to help my mom vomit the medication she ingested? Why was I so stupid?!* I was so angry with myself but didn't want my mom to see it. She already had enough going on, and I didn't want her to be concerned about me.

As the weeks went by, my mom was finally released after no longer being deemed a danger to herself. She came home with a lightness in her spirit, and then something set her off, and she returned to her usual old ways. There was a part of me that hoped that her experience in the psychiatric unit would scare her to the point of not wanting to try to harm herself. But I was awfully wrong. My stomach sank every time she started making comments about wanting to disappear or die. I knew that, eventually, her words would become actions and that I would have to figure out how to stop it or how to fix it once she did what she did. This created a level of anxiety and stress that I wish upon nobody, not even my worst enemy. This kind of anxiety and stress consumed me internally. The experiences destroyed me on the inside, but on the outside, I remained composed. I couldn't emotionally connect to the experience because I wouldn't be able to think or figure things out properly and quickly.

Several trips later to the psychiatric unit earned my mom a record. Her psychiatric hospitalizations followed her to every medical appointment, ambulance call, and outpatient clinic walk-in. I saw the interactions between the doctors and my mom change from concerned to now looking at her with the "here we go again" eyes. There were a few times that I interjected during her conversations with doctors because they were dismissing what she was trying to explain to them. I questioned why they weren't calling to run exams or further investigate her presenting concerns. The doctors would often give me a look of annoyance but would eventually run the exams to further evaluate my mom. My mom spoke, but it seemed like she no longer had a voice. So, I became her voice.

It was October 2010, and my mom had been hospitalized due to chest pains that she was experiencing at the time. I was helping my former boss organize her daughter's first birthday party when I received a call from my stepfather, Rodrigo, telling me that she was in the hospital. I was at a crossroads. I was in New Jersey, having a list of things to do to help set up the venue for the birthday party. Rodrigo told me that he wasn't sure what was going on with my mom just yet but that she was admitted while the doctors ran exams. A part of me was concerned, and another part of me thought that this was just like every other time. She would go to the hospital, stay for a few days, and then come home. Ironically, I was judging the doctors for disregarding my mom based on her history, but here I was doing the exact same thing. I defended my mom against this very biased perspective, yet here I was, desensitized to her as well. I felt the pressure of responsibility sink in and made the decision to finish setting up the venue and then go to the hospital afterward.

It was nighttime when I arrived at the hospital, and visiting hours were almost over. My mom and Rodrigo were in the room. I asked about what happened, and he explained that the doctors believed that she had suffered a minor heart attack. I suddenly felt my heart sink. A heart attack? How could this be possible?! All of the previous times that she was hospitalized were either due to surgeries, suicide attempts, or her usual complaints of pain. But none of her hospitalizations were due to something as real as a heart attack! Minor or not, it was still a heart attack. I looked at my mom and asked whether she was okay. She looked at me tiredly and said that she was okay but was going to try to sleep because she didn't have energy. I felt like the worst person in the world. I chose a birthday party over my mother, who needed me. It is to this day that this experience haunts me. My people-pleasing tendency surpassed another level, and my desensitization surpassed a new low. Who was I? What had I become?

A few days passed, and my mother seemed to be feeling better. It was morning time, and I was on my way to work, waiting for the infamous bus that you guys read about in Chapter 1, when I got a call from my mom. She whispered and told me that I had to call the hospital because the doctors wanted to transfer her to the psychiatric unit. I was confused and thought that perhaps my mom misunderstood what the doctors had told her. She then spoke sternly and said that she understood perfectly that they were going to transfer her to the psychiatric unit. I asked her why, and she said that she had no clue. Well, if she had no clue, then how was I supposed to know why she was being transferred? I still felt that there must have been some miscommunication, and I assured her there was no reason for the doctors to transfer her. She started to beg me to please not let them transfer her, and I told her to be patient and wait to speak to the doctors again. She asked me if I could call the social worker, and I told her I would call her later because I was on my way to work. She abruptly said fine and ended the call. I was a bit concerned but still sure that my mom must have misunderstood the doctors. A few hours later, Rodrigo called to tell me that my mom had been transferred to the psychiatric unit of the hospital.

I became filled with rage and confusion. What the hell was she doing in the psychiatric unit if she was admitted initially due to symptoms of a heart attack?! My thoughts began to race, and I started to have cold sweats. All I kept telling myself was to think. *Think, Lindsay, think!* I tried calling the hospital several times, but it just kept going directly to voicemail. I became increasingly frustrated because there was no reasonable explanation as to why this was happening. I was angry with the hospital, but I was more angry with myself! Why didn't I believe my mom when she told me that the doctors were going to transfer her?! Why didn't I try to call the social worker right away? Why did I, again, put something else before my mom? What kind of daughter was I?!

By the time I reached the hospital, the visiting hours had already ended, and I couldn't help but cry from despair. I met up with

Rodrigo and asked him about what was going on. He told me that the doctors felt that they had to transfer her based on her previous psychiatric hospitalizations to ensure that she was not a danger to herself. I looked at him and literally screamed, "What?! What kind of bullshit was that?!" If there was ever a time in which I wanted to burn a building down to the ground, it was definitely this time. This was an injustice that was being committed against my mom, and there was no plausible reason for them to have transferred her in the first place. I barely slept that night and felt horrible. I felt guilty because, once again, I let my mom down. Once again, I wasn't there to protect her. I felt that I had let her down and had become like the world and disregarded her.

The morning time came, and as soon as 9:00 a.m. hit, I began calling the hospital. Many calls later, I finally received a call back from the social worker, who kindly told me that she wasn't able to release any patient-related information because there was no signed consent from my mom. By this time, my patience was out the window, and I demanded an appointment with the psychiatric team that was in charge of my mom. The social worker obliged and gave me an appointment for the following day. I was mortified that my mom, once again, had to relive her hell in that unit. I called her and spoke to her briefly, and I assured her that I was going to fix this. She simply said okay and asked me to please get her out of there. Hearing those words felt like a dagger to my heart because I knew an injustice was being committed against her, and I didn't believe her when she initially told me that she was being transferred.

The following day came, and all I could think about was this meeting. Directly after work, I headed to the hospital, and as soon as I stepped out of the train station, cats and dogs started to fall from the sky. Not literally, but it sure looked like it! The rain poured and seemed to get heavier by the second. I looked at my watch and realized I only had a few minutes left before the meeting. With no umbrella, I stepped out of the train station and ran as fast as I could. I ran for approximately 6-7 minutes in the downpour, and by the time I reached the lobby, I was completely soaked. I squeezed my shirt and sweater by the garbage bin, and I could hear every step I made with my squeaky sneakers. Drenched from top to bottom, I approached the security desk and reported that I had a meeting in the psychiatric unit. I was asked to sit and wait until the social worker came to get me. As I sat in the waiting room, dripping wet, I felt an interesting serenity. I didn't feel rage. I didn't feel guilty. I felt nothing. I felt numb. I had an apple inside the pocket of my sweater that I was planning to give to my mom once she was finally released to me. I went to the meeting with every intention of leaving with my mom afterward.

Minutes later, the social worker finally arrived and escorted me upstairs. Prior to letting me in, she looked at me and said that I looked too young to be attending this meeting alone. I looked at her as the water dripped down my forehead and told her that I was 20 years old and was quite capable of attending this meeting on my own. She then quickly looked down and walked me to the conference room. I sat down at the head of this long table surrounded by six staff members. At the start of the conversation, their tone was dismissive and condescending, almost like how one would speak to a kid. However, that quickly changed when I asked direct questions and continued to ask them to elaborate on their ambiguous answers.

I presented my mom's case in a way that a lawyer would present their client's case. I provided and confirmed her history in the unit and expanded on the presenting problem that caused her to be admitted. I then asked for the plausible evidence that they had in order to determine that she was a risk to herself. They reported that during one of the lab exams, her blood levels showed high levels of a medication that contained methadone. They explained that this caused them to believe that she was overdosing on her medication. I looked at them and asked for the name of the medication. Inside of my pocket were several bottles of my mom's medications that I had brought in as evidence. (Side note: I grew up watching court shows, and if there was one thing that I learned, it was to make sure you always had evidence to prove your case!) I took out the medication bottle in question and showed them that the bottle was practically full. I asked them if my mom was, in fact, overdosing on this medication, wouldn't the bottle have fewer pills based on the medication frequency? They quickly said that they couldn't count the pills to confirm that this was the case. I told them that it was not a problem for me to count the pills for them.

Pill by pill, I counted until I reached the very last one, and I then did the math for them based on the prescribed frequency of the medication. The room became quiet, and as I looked into the faces of the doctors, I asked them, "Is there anything else that you would like for me to help clarify?" One of the doctors reported that they were going to review the case and make the decision of when to discharge her. I abruptly interjected and told them that no further review was necessary and that they had already made this experience sufficiently disturbing. I demanded that my mom be released immediately to me. One of the doctors sighed and looked at me for a few seconds. He then told me that they would have to process her discharge the following day because it was already too late in the day.

I compromised and agreed to her discharge for the following day. I know you may be thinking that my position seemed a bit arrogant and entitled, but I felt like I had to become this kind of person in order to be seen, heard, and taken seriously. If I had gone through this exact situation and reacted to them with a timid and polite demeanor, I am not sure that they would have taken me seriously or given me the time of day.

I asked to see my mom before leaving. As soon as I saw my mom, I hugged her. I asked her if she was okay, and she just nodded her head and looked down. I told her that I was getting her out of there but that she just had to spend one more night there. I asked her if she had eaten, and she said no. I then went up to one of the doctors who was in the meeting, and I told him that I wanted to give my mother an apple, but I knew it was not allowed. I explained that she was hungry and had not been able to eat. He looked at my mom and looked at me. He whispered to me to take my mom into the conference room and have her eat the apple very quickly while he stayed in the hallway as a lookout. I took my mom by the arm, walked fast inside the conference room, and gave her the apple to eat. I rushed her and told her that she would never step foot into another psychiatric ward again after this experience. My mom finished her apple and went back out into the common area. I thanked the doctor and left. I felt grateful because he chose to be human first.

As I walked out of the hospital, I felt a sense of accomplishment and relief. But for some reason, I still felt like I had let my mom down. It was only one more night, but it was one whole night of hell for her. Why did all of this have to happen? I felt responsible for not believing her in the first place and not being there in time to protect her. I felt like the weight of the world was on my shoulders, yet I couldn't allow myself to process the emotions from this experience. I continued to numb myself because I didn't have the time or energy to focus on Lindsay. Lindsay was not a priority; my mom was the priority. I left Lindsay inside that cave because I had to continue being the fighter that my mom needed me to be. I was my mother's keeper.

Chapter 4

THE FIRST TIME I WALKED INTO HER DARKNESS

Has there ever been a time when you acted out of impulse or in a way that could be considered irrational or unusual compared to how you would normally react? Has there ever been a time in which you have said or done hurtful things to others that you later regretted? If you have answered yes to either of these questions, then that certifies that you, too, are human, and sometimes we need gentle reminders of this. There are times when it becomes easier to point the finger or judge others based on their actions without remembering that we are all humans and make mistakes. There are times in which our distress becomes so great that we act in ways that don't make sense to others, but for you, it may provide temporary relief. Sometimes, we can also become so wrapped up in labeling things as right or wrong that we tend to forget that behind our actions lies a world of emotions and distorted perceptions that can lead us to act out in ways that may be perceived as irrational by those on the outside.

I was about 8-years old when I started to see my mom in a very different light. It was Saturday, and I was home with my mom and brothers while my dad was at work. I remember that this was around the time that computers started to become more accessible and popular in homes. My dad had brought home one of his work computers. I was so curious about its capabilities and enjoyed playing with the keyboard and hearing the keys click away. On this particular day, I was messing with the keyboard, and the monitor went black. I tried to restart the computer, but it didn't work, so my immediate reaction was to run and tell my mom that the computer had inexplicably shut off. I knew that if anyone could help, it'd be her. After all, she *was* a mom! She went to the living room where the computer was and began pressing buttons, trying to get it to work. Unfortunately for me, my mom's "magic" seemed to be not working because the computer did not turn back on after numerous attempts.

"What did you do?!" My mom looked at me angrily, and of course, like any other kid in my shoes, I denied any involvement. After a few minutes of me continuing to lie, my mom became more impatient and frustrated. "Go to my room now!" she yelled. I slowly went, and she followed behind. I could feel her energy starting to get a hold of me. I wasn't sure what was going to happen, but I knew that I was in trouble. As I walked into the room, I stood by her bed, and as I turned to face her, I saw that she had closed the door.

"Ah, crap! Here we go!" I thought to myself. I didn't know if she was going to yell at me or hit me. Whatever was about to happen, I knew that she didn't want my brothers to know. As my mom approached me, I could see in her eyes that she was angry. By this time, I felt scared. I hadn't seen my mom like this before. Sure, I had been hit a few times in the past, but this time, there was something different about her. I looked up into her eyes and saw so much anger coming out. As she began to talk to me in a stern tone, her pupils seemed to have enlarged, and her eyes appeared darker. She, once again, started interrogating me about the computer and wanted to know why I'd touched it in the first place. She alluded to the fact that my dad was going to be really upset, although I knew better.

My dad was typically understanding, calm, and loving. His punishments consisted of lectures about how he was so disappointed and how my brothers and I (or whoever was the culprit at the time) needed to do better. Sometimes, his lectures were more painful than the belt whoopings, but whatever the repercussions of an action were, I thought they would be mild. Was I wrong? Why else would my mom behave this way if my dad wouldn't get mad? After a while, I confessed and began to apologize. I told her that the whole situation was an accident. Before I knew it, my mom pushed me against the wall and proceeded to wrap her hands around my throat and choke me.

It felt like an eternity, but it was only a few seconds where I couldn't breathe. As Mom's grip around my neck became tighter, I looked directly into her eyes with tears rolling down my cheeks and gently tapped her hands as a plea to be released. She eventually released her grip, and her pupils returned to normal almost instantly. I touched my neck as I took my first breath of air and coughed a bit. I said nothing at that moment but remembered feeling scared. I didn't know what had just happened. I didn't realize that what I did warranted such a punishment. I bowed my head down because, at that moment, I wasn't sure if my punishment was over. I wasn't sure what would happen next. My mother quickly told me that I could not mention this to anyone and that if I did, I would be in greater trouble. I instantly knew that I had to keep my mouth shut, and there was nothing in me that wanted to defy my mom because of my fear of having this kind of punishment happen again. She then opened the door and told me to go to the living room. I remained quiet for the rest of the day and sat on the couch watching television. I didn't want to touch anything, and I didn't want to say anything that would once again upset her.

My dad arrived home from work later that evening, and as my mom calmly explained to him that something was wrong with the computer, he quickly was able to fix it, and once again, the computer was in working order. Mom never told Dad that I had almost broken it earlier in the day, and I assumed that she was trying to protect me from being punished by him. After all, she did say that he would be really upset. Perhaps on this occasion, my dad would've reacted differently; at least, that's what she seemed to want to convince me of. I never questioned whether it was normal or not to choke your child as a form of punishment. I wasn't sure what to make of the situation, so I decided to disregard it as being a one-time thing. However, unbeknownst to me, this situation set a precedent for what was yet to come. Things escalated from moments when she lost control to moments when I could see in her eyes that she wanted me dead. I wish I could tell you that this was the only time that something like this happened; that my mother became so angry with me that it felt like she wanted me gone. I think at this age, a part of me wanted to remain in denial that there was something wrong with the way she reacted to me. The truth is that this was one of many times in which she lost control. This was one of many times in which she looked at me as her target. Sometimes, it felt like she saw me as her enemy. But this was my mom. How could any of this make sense?

Years later, a similar experience happened between me and her. But this time, it felt more volatile. This time, it felt more personal, and I could see in her eyes, just like I did years before, that she wanted me gone. I was in my teens at this time, and my mom and I were having a discussion that quickly escalated into an argument. But not the kind of argument where you can agree to disagree. I remember trying to reason with her and explain my point of view as calmly as possible. I felt frustrated and as though she was making absolutely no effort to listen to me. The argument soon escalated into something beyond my imagination. As I stood in the living room, she stormed into the kitchen, and I immediately heard her shuffling through the kitchen drawer. This could only mean one thing: she was going to try to slit her wrists. Again.

Boy, was I wrong this time!

When she came out of the kitchen, she, in fact, did have a knife in her hand, but the knife was pointed at me. As she walked closer to me, my heart started racing because I had not experienced this before. What was I supposed to do? Should I run? Should I try to reason with her? I looked at her and looked at the kitchen knife in disbelief. There was no way that my own mother could be possibly pulling out a knife ON HER OWN DAUGHTER!

As she walked towards me, I had the sudden realization that this was very much true and actually happening. Initially, it started with me pleading with her and trying to wake her up from whatever trance she was in. I vividly remember her eyes turning dark, like in the first incident when she choked me.

I knew that during these incidents, I wasn't before my mom. I didn't know this person. Her energy felt dark, and it felt like I was in front of a monster instead. My adrenaline would always pump, my heart would race, and there was always a cold sweat down my back. Was this the end for me? Luckily for me, my older brother, Raymie, was around and physically got in the middle of us while pushing her away from me. I didn't make any sudden movements in an effort to not startle her. The seconds felt like minutes, and the minutes felt like hours. When would this end? And more importantly, how?

Raymie eventually convinced her to release the knife to him. These kinds of situations happened numerous times where my mom would lose control and try to take it out on me, and Raymie would come to my rescue. I never have and never will forget these moments of courage and bravery. While Raymie stood between us, I also had Raylin on standby. But being that he was my baby brother, I never wanted him to get involved because Raymie and I felt like his protectors. We could take the brunt of situations as long as nothing affected him. No matter how scary and dark things got, I knew that I could always count on both of my brothers because we stood together through thick and thin. We have defended each other unconditionally, without hesitation or even a second thought. I am thankful to be able to experience this journey of life with them because they have made it bearable and totally worth it. My brothers are how I know that unconditional love does, in fact, exist.

There were other times when I wasn't as lucky to have my brothers around, and it would just be my mom and me. The first few times, I again would try to reason with her and wake her up from the trance of rage that she seemed to be transported to. Eventually, either the phone would ring, which would startle her enough to back off, or she would simply tell me to prepare myself because there would be a next time. Fear is all I knew at this time. I didn't know how or when things would get better, but I understood that as long as I was under my mother's roof, very little would change. I would sometimes find my heart racing while I was sitting on the couch watching TV, as if I was in the middle of danger. It became normal for me to feel scared a lot of the time, even when nothing was happening. It became normal for me until it wasn't. Until I grew weary and tired, at which time I would accept defeat and not even attempt to discourage my mom from whatever she was about to do to me at that moment.

As I stood in front of her, yet again, with a knife in her hands, I no longer felt scared. The dark, monstrous eyes that used to cause me panic no longer had the same effect. In fact, I looked into her eyes and felt nothing. I felt nothing to the extent that I actually wanted her to go through with whatever she wanted to do to me because I figured that at least she would take me out of my misery. I figured if this was the last time she pulled out a knife on me and killed me, then I wouldn't have to worry about anticipating these kinds of events. And I would no longer be in a state of stress, worry, and fear. There were times when I even approached her and told her to simply do it and get it over with. I noticed that there was a shift. The experience shifted from her having control of the situation by instilling fear in me to now her taking a step back and visibly reconsidering what she was doing. My physical, emotional, mental, and spiritual exhaustion took the power away from her because I was no longer that frightened child. I was simply too tired to give a fuck!

It took many years before I realized that what I had experienced was not the norm. It took me even longer to realize that what I had endured with my mother was actually called abuse. Sitting with this concept didn't sit well with me. Why would my mom ever want to abuse or hurt me? Our mothers are supposed to protect us, not hurt us. The effects of my experiences and abuse trickled in very subtly. So subtly that it was not until my early adulthood, after my mom was no longer alive, that I felt this immense void and pain that hit me like a bag of bricks. I had never felt so alone and detached from the world as I had felt in the first few years after my mother's death. I often thought to myself, *Why should I be here? If someone like my mother, who was supposed to love and protect me, was able to hurt me this way and sometimes even make me feel as though she wanted me dead, then why should I still be here?*

This question led me to sink deeper and deeper into my depression. It led me to feel hopeless, disconnected, and detached from the world. I was existing but not really living. I felt like I was a walking dead person who often felt guilty for taking up space that someone else could probably use better. Once I arrived home and took off the mask that I put on every day for the world to see, I would lay in my bed and cry. I cried from pain. I cried from frustration. I cried from anger. Sometimes, I even cried internally because the tears would no longer come out. If I had to label this experience as anything, I would label it as a death sentence because that's how it felt.

Years ago, I had learned to believe that there was something wrong with me. And that I wasn't enough. I learned that it was my job to make others happy, to make my mother happy. However, no matter my efforts and attempts, for some reason, people would eventually walk out of my life. This idea of abandonment led me to believe that I had to be more than just myself. I had to work really hard to impress people or keep them content. I felt like I needed a purpose in people's lives; otherwise, why would they want me around? This, of course, trickled into most, if not all, of my relationships with people, whether it was friendships or romantic relationships. And every time a relationship ended, I looked at myself in the mirror, feeling more worthless with every passing minute.

That's the thing about perception. You can always find evidence to prove and validate your story. We are all authors of our stories. We often narrate our stories based on our perception of reality, and what I have come to realize is that sometimes, our perceived reality is different from the actual reality. For example, when you're feeling really sad or down, the things you pay attention to or experience may very well intensify or add to your current experience of sadness. Sometimes, with enough time, our perception can become distorted, and we can interpret experiences from a limited point of view. This is not to say that you have a wrong or right perception of things. It simply means that when we experience these uncomfortable or unpleasant emotions, it can become that much more challenging to see the bigger picture or to see things from a different perspective. Our emotions can sometimes lead us to see things in a limited kind of way compared to when we are feeling uplifted and encouraged.

For many years, I narrated my story as the girl whose mother didn't love her. I painted a picture that had me separated from the world. I was an outsider. I didn't belong. I compared myself to others and saw them happy and living the life I wished I had. Lives filled with loving partners and families that didn't abandon them. My story was that I often put other people's needs ahead of mine and would go above and beyond for them so that they wouldn't abandon me. However, in the end, the outcome seemed to play out the same, and each time, I became more depleted than the last. This was the point when I came to terms with my reality and accepted my fate. I believed that some people came into this world and got everything they wanted, while there were others, like me, who would simply never attain such a life. A life of love. A life where I was enough. A life where I felt complete. That's the funny thing about growing up yearning for your mother's love; I have learned that I placed the expectation on others to give me the love and acceptance that I was looking for from her. My happiness, my self-worth, and my peace all relied on the external world, as I didn't even know how to give these things to myself. I thought that as long as I was working hard, going to school, and continued to keep pushing, there would come a time when someone would walk into my life and provide all these things for me, and boy, was I wrong!

Time and time again, my relationships would head down very similar paths, and I couldn't understand why. What was it about me that people seemed to not want to stay in my life? During my second experience in therapy, several years after my mom passed away, I started to open my eyes to a different reality, to a different perspective. I was told that all those desires and expectations that I had for other people were actually things that I had to fulfill for myself. "But how?" I asked. How in the world could I provide these things for myself? I felt empty and deserted inside and didn't even know where to begin. And thus, the work began, and it still hasn't stopped.

The path to self-discovery is a path that is anything but easy. It is a path that requires you to look at your strengths and your weaknesses and embrace them all with love, understanding, and compassion. It forces you to remove the bandages and expose your wounds as they open up and begin to bleed once again. I've learned that throughout my life, I didn't know and didn't want to confront the emotions and internal demons that every experience brought forth, so I simply put them away and continued moving forward in hopes that they would not return. I have learned that in focusing so much of my energy on my mom and everything else going on, I never truly learned how to do the same for myself. Instead, those experiences led me to believe that someone else should have done for me as I did for my mom.

With therapy and the divine creatures that I get to call my friends and mentors, I have been able to learn how to invest that same energy in myself that I have tried to give to other people. It has not been an easy process, and there are still times I resort to my old habits, but it has been a liberating experience because my peace no longer relies on anything or anyone outside of me. The path to self-discovery has taught me to take responsibility for the things I can control: myself. It has placed the power back into my hands and shifted my perspective from being a victim of my circumstances to now being someone with many gifts to share with the world. That's the thing about life; it is through the most difficult experiences that we are not only able to learn more about ourselves but also able to learn how to sit with our emotions and listen to them. Because even in the darkest of times, and even through our pain, our emotions are there to shed light and help us find the answers that we are looking for.

My self-reflection and lessons up to this point have taught me more about my mom than I could have ever imagined. If I had known then what I know now, I think I would have seen her in a very different light. My mother, just like me, was yearning for a love she could not seem to find. She was yearning to feel complete and placed that responsibility on others. My mother, like me, narrated her storyline from the perspective of someone who felt helpless and in constant pain that no one seemed to be able to fix. Her emotional pain turned into physical pain, and she lived with the numbing effects of her medication until her body couldn't take it any longer. When I lived through the torment with her, I saw her as the enemy at times, as a monster, as someone that I could never please or be enough for. I look at my mom now as someone who was in a world of pain, waiting to be seen, waiting to be heard, waiting to feel all the things she didn't know how to provide for herself.

I see my mom as someone who honestly did the best she could despite all of her internal battles. There were times in which my mom was overprotective of my brothers and me. She defended us when people would try to say negative things about us. My grandmother would often say that my mother was like a lioness willing to do anything for her cubs. And I believe this is true. She tried to protect us from the world but just didn't know how to protect us from her when she lost control.

My experience with my mom taught me that we are all hurting to some capacity and that, many times, the way we act and react to others has very little to do with them and more to do with ourselves. Understanding this has allowed me to be just that more understanding. Before impulsively reacting to people's actions, I now try to take a step back and evaluate if this experience is really about me or if this is just a projection of the person's own internal battles. Approaching life from this perspective has not been easy, but it has also allowed me to let down my guard and not react so much from a defensive or impulsive perspective.

If I had the opportunity today to sit down with my mom, I would speak to her and acknowledge that I saw her, that I saw her pain, and that it was okay. I would tell my mom that I knew she was not her actions, and I knew that, inside, she was still there. Because all along, my mom was always there. She just needed some help returning to herself during the times she lost herself and her control.

Chapter 5

THE DIVORCE – THE HURT, LIES, &AFTERMATH

As a kid, I remember thinking that I had the perfect parents who never fought, loved each other, and always got along. I saw how much they supported each other, both professionally and personally. They seemed to have a great partnership because who they were as individuals seemed to complement their relationship. Anytime we went out as a family to a restaurant, a wedding, or a family gathering, I felt like my family was a picture-perfect family, and I grew up feeling lucky because I felt like they were my safety net. If there was ever a problem, they would have the answers to figure it out.

Typically, they were both in sync, and I could count on one hand the number of times I ever noticed any kind of tension between them. Unfortunately, though, when my mother started to experience increased health problems, their dynamic seemed to shift more and more. Much like my own experience, I felt like their relationship transitioned from being about the two of them to suddenly being mostly about my mom and her well-being. We were all focused on her health and wanted her to feel better. Surgery after surgery, I noticed that my dad's plate of responsibilities increased from having to tend to my mom at the hospital while still maintaining his job and taking care of my brothers and me. The days became longer, and there was a void in our home without my mom. Throughout it all, I don't remember ever having heard my dad complain that he was tired or that he needed help. If anything, he would remind my brothers and me that we had to pray for our mom's recovery and help her when she returned home from her surgeries.

"Together in sickness and in health." Those were the vows that my parents took when they married each other, and I felt like my dad was living up to his promise. I know that my mom's health affected how she viewed the world, and I believe it also affected how my parents looked at each other. On one end, my mom was overcome with her own health decline and post-recovery process after every surgery, but on the other end was my dad and the sense of loss of the partner he once had. They no longer laughed as much or talked as much in front of us. Instead, they tried to deal with both of their realities the best way they could. Looking back on everything now, I sincerely think that both my mom and dad tried their best to be there for each other through the good and the bad times, but there comes a time when an increase in hopelessness leads to an increase in disagreements and tension. In my opinion, this is what happened with my parents over time. It was not an abrupt or obvious change, but it was a subtle change that progressed over time until it blew up in everyone's face.

My parents never argued in front of my brothers and me, but after a while, we realized that when they closed their room door during the day, it was because they were having an argument. At first, this would only happen occasionally, but as the days went by, having the door closed during the daytime became more frequent, and I could feel in my stomach that something was off. I could see the tension in my parents' faces when they would open the room door. I didn't want to admit to myself or anyone else that there was a possibility that they were experiencing marital problems. This was mom and dad, and they had always been able to figure out their issues in the past. This time would be no different, right?

I remember one night when I was up late in the living room doing some homework. My brothers and mom had already gone to bed. My dad walked into the living room and sat next to me on the couch. He looked at me but didn't say anything. I looked at him and asked if everything was okay. He came closer, kissed me on my cheek, and, in a soft voice, said, "I want you to know that no matter what happens in this life, I will always love you, and you will always be my little girl." I looked at him and felt worried. *Why was he saying this to me right now? Was there something going on that I didn't know about? Was he also sick like Mom? Was he going to die?*

As I look back on this specific instance with my dad, I can't help but also think about the last time that I saw my mom alive. During our last interaction, her last words to me were, "I love you," and I remember having the same eerie feeling that something bad was going to happen. That's why, still today, I sometimes still struggle with being happy or appreciating the bliss that life has to offer. Being happy or feeling blissful scares the crap out of me because, in the instances that I felt this happiness, I soon plummeted to the ground with life's curve balls.

I looked at my dad the same way I looked at my mom before she passed away and asked, "Is everything ok?" I feared the truthful answer. Despite his tone, he found the strength to smile, "Everything is fine. I just wanted you to know that." I allowed myself to believe him beyond my gut feelings because I wanted to be wrong. I wanted to believe that this was just a randomized gesture and had no deeper meaning or symbolism.

As more time went by, the relationship my parents once had became more serious in nature. They went from spending time together with us to now spending more time with us individually. Our dinners became quieter, and I could feel that there was tension. There were times when my mom would say things to my dad, and he seemed irritable and short with his responses. *What the hell was going on here?* In my mind, if I didn't say or ask anything out loud, then it wouldn't be real. I just thought that this was a phase and that, eventually, things would go back to normal. This phase did seem to be taking longer than expected, but I was still hopeful that they would put their differences to the side and remember how much they loved each other.

The chances of my parents resolving their issues became slimmer and slimmer as time passed. I remember one evening, my grandma, brothers, and I were watching television in the living room and heard our parents' bedroom door swing open aggressively. We all quickly stood up to see what was happening. From the living room, I could hear my mom crying. As I looked into the room from where I was, I saw my mom sitting on one side of the bed while my dad lay down on the other side. My grandma and I rushed to their room, but she closed the door in front of me before I entered so that she could talk to my parents privately. Eavesdropping at the door, I overheard my mom saying, "He hit me."

I winced immediately. *What the hell was happening? Could it be true that my dad hit my mom? But my dad would never do something like that! Then why would my mom say that if it weren't true?* These were all of the conflicting thoughts and questions that overwhelmed my existence. Unfortunately, I couldn't hear anything else from the conversation, so I returned to the living room where my brothers remained, waiting for my grandma to come out and let us know what had happened.

The suspense was killing me! The minutes felt like hours, and I felt uneasy and nervous. The claim of abuse, whether physical or emotional, had never been brought up before. I prayed that this was just one big misunderstanding. The bedroom door finally opened again, and my brothers and I went to see what my grandma would say.

"Don't worry," she said. "Your parents were just having a small disagreement."

"Then why is mommy crying?" I asked while feeling confused.

"She is just upset."

As my grandma tried to continue to put on a brave face, my mom came out of the room and told my brothers and me the same words I overheard while eavesdropping, "Your dad hit me."

My brothers and I began to ask questions about why my dad would do such a thing, and my mom told us that he got upset with their conversation. I couldn't believe what my grandma or my mom were saying because, on the one hand, my grandma was telling us that everything was fine, and on the other hand, my mom was telling us that things were not fine, so I went into the room to ask my dad what had happened.

"I did not hit your mother."

Three people and three different stories. I didn't know who to believe or who to trust. My grandma didn't know what else to do, so she told my brothers and me to go to bed and that everything would be fine in the morning. We went to bed, but I couldn't believe the reality that I was living in. Why were my parents fighting like this? When were things going to go back to normal? Were we ever going to go back to normal?

The morning finally came, and I remember waking up early to see if I could talk to my dad before he left for work. It was the weekend, and when he saw me in the living room, he asked me if I wanted to go to work with him. I immediately said yes because I needed to know what happened the night before based on his perspective. I quickly got ready, and we headed to the train station. Nothing was said during our walk, but as we waited for the train, I turned to my dad and asked him if it was true what Mom had said. He looked at me with a serious but sad look on his face and, without giving me specifics, told me that he would never lay a finger on my mom, no matter how upset he was. He explained to me that while they were having an argument, he tried to walk away from my mom, but she wouldn't let him, and that is when she opened the door and accused him of hitting her.

He looked at me in my eyes the entire time and told me that he would also never lie to me. I didn't need to hear anything else because I already decided who to believe. In my heart, I believed my dad. The train came, and on our way to his job, I remember feeling a sigh of relief, but at the same time, I was worried. I didn't know how I could get my parents back to the way they were before, when they got along with one another.

The months went by, and my mom's physical health continued to deteriorate. Every time she returned home from a doctor's appointment, she seemed to have more medications added to her regimen. She slept more during the days, and when she was awake, I could see a deep sadness in her eyes. She wouldn't say anything about it but would attribute it to her back pain. Soon, it became the norm to see her in bed and see my dad become more distant from her. They slept in the same bed, but a part of me felt that it had all turned into a façade. The façade was up in 2002 when everything just hit the fan.

I was 11 years old and having an ordinary evening. I was taking a shower before getting ready to go to bed while my brothers were in the living room and my parents were in their bedroom. As I was finishing my shower, I heard a loud scream and things being thrown against a door. I quickly dried myself off and, in my towel, rushed out of the bathroom to see what was happening. As I opened the door, my dad abruptly opened the bedroom door to leave the room, and that's when I saw a bunch of shoes on the floor and my mom crying and screaming at my dad. I asked them what was going on, and no one answered me. My brothers also went to the room to see what was happening, but my mom just kept crying and told us how much our dad had hurt her. *What was she talking about?* I thought to myself.

My dad quickly returned to the bedroom and grabbed his already-packed luggage. I was in shock because everything was fine during the day. Things were rocky at times, but I didn't think that they were this bad. My dad waited for us in the living room with his luggage to say goodbye. My brothers and I were in the room with my mom when she started to tell us all sorts of things about my dad and how much of a bad person he was. She even told Raymie how my dad never wanted him to be born. She explicitly told him that my dad tried to convince her to get an abortion, but she didn't want to. Raymie was about 14 years old at the time, and to hear something like that at that age was cruel and perhaps even inhumane. How much pain she must have been in to want to cause the same amount of pain within us. I looked at my mom in disbelief about everything that was coming out of her mouth because my dad was not the horrible person that she was telling us about.

As my dad was getting ready to leave, my mom told us to go say goodbye to him because he was leaving us. We went to my dad, where I hugged him so tightly and started to cry. I told him that I didn't want him to leave. He looked at us and told us that he had no choice but to leave and that he would see us again soon. He told us to listen to our mom and continue to do well in school. I looked into his watery eyes and could feel his pain. He gave us one final hug and then left. As the door closed behind him, we went back to the room to sit with our mom, and this is when our hell began. As we sat with her, she continued to tell us what a horrible person my dad was. The person in front of me was a completely different person than who I knew my mother to be. She seemed to be filled with so much hate and resentment toward my dad. Why? All these years, they seemed happy together, and now my dad was gone, and my mom was bashing his name. After she was done releasing everything she had pent up inside, she told us to go to bed.

I went to bed and felt like I was living a nightmare that I just wanted to wake up from. *What would tomorrow look like? Could it be any worse than what it already was?* I didn't know the answer, but I was becoming hopeless that things could ever go back to any kind of normal after all of this.

From that moment on, we experienced a different side of my mom that I had never experienced before. She became unpredictable, impulsive, and irrational. I felt like I had to walk on eggshells now because I was afraid to do or say anything that would upset her, which would have probably led to another one of her uproars.

One day, my mom told us that she and my dad were getting divorced. I didn't know what life would look like now that my parents were no longer together and now that my mom was literally bouncing off the walls. We had not seen my dad for some time, and my mom insisted that it was because he didn't care about us. I felt like I was living in chaos and constant turmoil. Things seemed to be going okay during their divorce until my mom decided that she wanted to have full custody of my brothers and me.

As she tried to build up her case, accusations and restraining orders started. During one of their court hearings, my mom had alleged that my dad physically hit her and also raped her on multiple occasions. I didn't know the details of the accusations until I learned that my dad had been arrested. I was living in hell because I knew that my mom was lying, but I couldn't say anything. I tried to reason with her, but she was determined. She was determined to make my dad feel the pain that she was clearly experiencing. Any time I would question her about it, she misconstrued some of our experiences when we were one happy family. She told us how our dad wanted to paint himself as a perfect, good guy but was the exact opposite.

The more she spoke, the less I believed her. This man she was describing was not my dad. And right about now, I saw her as a monster. Throughout my dad's multiple arrests, my aunt, my mom's sister, was there and helped bail him out. She also couldn't believe what my mom was doing. We all saw what she was doing but felt so powerless because she could call the police at any given time and tell them another lie about my dad just to get him arrested once again.

After my dad was bailed out, my mom requested a restraining order against him. She told the court that she was in fear that he would retaliate and didn't want my dad to have access to her or us. The judge approved the restraining order, and we were not allowed to see or talk to my dad. Hell seemed to be getting worse by the day, and I didn't know what the outcome of all of this would be. One afternoon, my mom seemed to be in good spirits and was very chatty with my brothers and me. She started to talk about my dad, but surprisingly, she wasn't saying any of her usual negative things about him. The topic of my friend's party came up. I wanted to go, and she told me that I didn't have any new clothes to wear. I shrugged it off and told her that it was okay and that I would just wear whatever I had in the closet. She told me that I deserved to have new clothes and told me to call my dad to ask him for money. I looked at her like she had three heads and reminded her of our restraining order. She assured me that it was okay and that she wouldn't tell anyone about this. She asked me to call my dad and ask him for $300 to buy new clothes. I told her that I didn't need that much money for clothes, and she told me to ask and see how much money he could give me.

Beyond my better judgment, I believed in the good in my mom at that moment, so I decided to oblige and call my dad. As soon as I heard his voice, I felt so happy because I hadn't spoken to or seen him in months since his previous arrests (by this time, my dad had already been arrested twice due to my mom's allegations). I asked him how he was doing, and he asked if my mom was around me. She obviously overheard what he was asking and signaled for me to say no. As I said no, I looked at my mom and saw her getting excited. I felt like perhaps she was going to be nice this time and let me talk to my dad without using it against him. My dad reminded me that we weren't supposed to be talking because of the restraining order, but he felt so happy to hear my voice. He told me to keep the conversation short in case my mom walked in on me. I explained to him that I needed new clothes and asked if he could give me $300. As soon as I said the amount, I told him that it was okay if he didn't have that much and that he could give me whatever amount he could. Without hesitation, he agreed but asked how he could get it to me. I told him that I would think about it and call him back. I hung up the phone and told my mom that he was going to give me the money but didn't know how to give it to me because of the restraining order. She told me not to worry and that she would take me to his office. She told me to call him back and tell him that I was going to stop by to pick up the money. I again reminded my mom about the restraining order, and she told me not to worry about it because she wasn't going to say anything to anyone. I called my dad back to tell him that I would be stopping by his office alone to pick up the money. He sounded nervous and told me that he would be taking a risk by doing this because if my mom found out, she could get him arrested again. I assured my dad that she wouldn't find out about it, and I hung up the phone. My mom then hugged me and told me to get dressed.

On our way to his office, I was both excited and scared to death because I had not seen my mom this happy in such a long time. She had already done so much to him in the past several months. What led to her sudden change of heart? I went inside his office alone and assured him that my mom was not with me. We hugged each other tightly for a few minutes. I told him that I missed him so much, and he told me that he also really missed me and that he was working hard to be able to see my brothers and me again soon. He then gave me the money and told me that I shouldn't stay long in case my mom noticed that I was not home. I thanked him and gave him one final hug before leaving.

As soon as I left the office and met up with my mom again, she asked that I give her the money. I asked her what store we were going to, and she told me that we had to stop by our home first. I didn't think much of it because I felt so relieved that I was able to see my dad and that mom was finally acting normal again.

This "normal" was short-lived because as soon as we got home, she called the police to report that my dad had violated the restraining order. I could not believe what I was seeing and hearing! I became so scared and begged her to please not do it. I begged her to please call the police back and tell them that she was lying. But despite all of my efforts, she went through with it. The police arrived shortly after to take her statement, and as I sat on the couch quietly, one of the officers approached me and said, "Look what you did to your pops." These words have forever remained ingrained in my heart because I couldn't believe that I did this to my own father! I felt like I was living through a slow death. This could not be my life right now, and yet it was.

My mom accompanied the officers who arrested my dad. My mom got back home and boasted about how she was in the car watching as my dad was handcuffed and his legs shackled while he was taken to the precinct for booking. As she described the experience, it seemed to bring her so much pleasure and joy. Meanwhile, I felt like a traitor and a liar. I felt disgusting because I let her use me in her little game, and now my dad was paying the consequences. I never knew what happened to the money that my dad had given me because it had gone directly into the hands of my mom. It was definitely not used to buy me any clothes.

If there was ever a time in which I wished my mother was dead, this was one of those moments. She was no longer my mom. She was an evil person who bled hate and malice. I didn't recognize her, and yet this was who I had to listen to. The court hearings continued, and time after time, I continued to listen to all of the different narratives of how my mom was the victim of my dad's ongoing abuse. Eventually, my mom allowed my brothers and I to have court-supervised visitations with my dad. We saw my dad for about a year or two under supervision until he decided to move back to the Dominican Republic. He told us that we could call him as many times as we wanted but that he had to try to get as far away from our mom before she got him arrested again.

Truth is, I didn't blame him for leaving because I also wanted to run away from her. I needed to know that my dad was safe and that she could no longer get to him, even if it meant that we wouldn't see him for some time. I knew my brothers and I were living in hell with my mom, but there was no need for my dad to be in hell with us anymore. What lay ahead felt like a death sentence because my mom's wrath and erratic behaviors only got worse over time.

I remember a time when I was already in high school, and my mom had asked me to call my aunt, her sister, to borrow one of her name-brand purses. By this time, no one trusted my mom, including her own family. I knew that my mom would probably not return the purse and then blame it on me, so I tried to make up an excuse to not have to call. My mom insisted, so I took the landline phone into the hallway and pretended to call my aunt. I knew if I had asked my aunt, she would say yes, and eventually, all of this would turn into a shitshow for me. I wanted to avoid this whole ordeal.

After a couple of minutes, I returned to the living room and told my mom that my aunt had said no and thought this would be the end of the conversation. To my surprise, my mom took the phone out of my hand, called my aunt, and asked if I had called her. My aunt told her no because she obviously had no idea what was going on. My mom then hung up the phone and started to hit me on my head and back while shouting nasty things at me. My only instinct at this time was to try to cover my face. She continued to hit me until she was tired. While getting beat, I remember just thinking, *When will this be over?* Not the situation but my life. I wanted my life to be over because I saw it as the only way to escape my mom. Again, this all just felt like I was dying a slow death because this would just be one of many other experiences when my mom lost all control and saw me as her target.

On a different occasion, I had just arrived home from work and was trying to pour myself a bowl of cereal to eat for dinner. I remember being so hungry because I had not eaten much during the day. As I went to pour the milk into the bowl, I lost grip on the carton, and all of the milk spilled on the floor. As I watched the milk spew out of the container, I remember feeling depleted because, yes, I was hungry and tired, but also because I just didn't enjoy living anymore.

As I went to clean up the milk from the floor, my mom stormed into the kitchen and started shouting at me."Calm down," I told her. "I am already cleaning it up!" I think I might as well have cursed at her because she decided to take the mop and repeatedly hit me over the head while still screaming at me. I was so confused because I didn't know why I had become her punching bag and why she found it so easy to beat me for every little mistake that I made.

This fear and sense of inadequacy reminded me of the 5-year-old Lindsay who was scared shitless after getting in trouble in kindergarten for breaking a rule. I felt like I couldn't make a mistake, and I started to blame myself for my mom's reactions. If she was upset, it was because of what I had done. When I have sat down to reflect and evaluate my previous relationships with people, as an adult, I can still see that little girl trying to be picture-perfect for fear of others' reactions to my mistakes. I've had to do a lot of digging and reflecting to understand that I am not and will not ever be responsible for people's actions or reactions, no matter who they are. I have tolerated a lot from people, including my mom, because I thought that was how love was shown. I thought I had to tolerate people's actions and reactions because every time I would try to tell my family about the hell that I was living through at home, their response would almost always be that I had to understand that my mom was sick and didn't know what she was doing. They justified her actions and behaviors, which then left me feeling like this was how life was supposed to look and feel.

Looking back at this time, I can acknowledge and validate the different hells my brothers, Mom, Dad, and I lived. If you asked all of us for each of our versions of events, you would end up with 5 different versions, not because anyone was lying but because this was how we interpreted our reality based on our own experiences and perceptions. My mom was absolutely living in a deep kind of hell, where she didn't know how to get out and felt like the world was against her. But I couldn't see it this way when I was living through it. I could only see my hell because everywhere I turned, I was being told that I had to understand my mom's situation. In all of this, not once did anyone think that my brothers and I were in danger, which many times we were. Not once did anyone ever try to take us out of our reality. It was almost as though this was the norm. We experienced all this turmoil, but no one acknowledged the seriousness of it all.

We are no longer living in this hell, but I can't help but continue to feel the effects of everything. It has taken me a very long time not to resent my family because there were so many people who were aware of what was going on with my brothers and me and did little to nothing to help us. We were kids and left to fend for ourselves while everyone on the outside pretended this was normal. The exterior and mistrust of people that I eventually developed was collateral from all of these experiences. For a long time, I have felt like I couldn't rely on or trust anyone to help me. Today, I am trying to put down this narrative with love for the exterior that I had to build, which served me a great deal of purpose and kept me alive in a lot of questionable situations.

When I think back at how I felt towards my mom during the time of their divorce, I remember feeling angry, confused, and hateful towards her. I hated the things that she tried to push me to believe. I hated that she hated my dad so much that there were times when she would even consider doing what we call "Brujeria," also known as witchcraft, on him. I hated everything about my mom at this time because I could not understand or rationalize why her whole being had taken such a drastic shift. The person I lived with during this time wasn't my mother. I couldn't recognize her. She was full of so much darkness and malice. There were times in which I wished that she would simply die. I wanted her to die because, at least then, she couldn't hurt my dad anymore. I had these thoughts, and when I verbalized them to my dad, he simply looked at me and said, "I know you're upset and hurting, but your mom is not okay right now."

Even during a time when Dad could've and should've hated her, he didn't. He didn't like her very much, but he never spoke hate towards her. Years after my mom had passed away, I made a comment to my former therapist during a session. I told her how there were so many times in my life that I honestly prayed and wished for my mother to die. I wanted her gone because I had lost hope that she could be my mom once again. With sad eyes, my therapist asked me a question that I answered with quite a bit of confidence. She asked me, "Now that your mom is gone, do you regret having said and wished for these things?" I looked her directly in the eyes and said, "No."

"I don't have regret for ever having wished or having said these things about my mom because at the time when I felt this way, my feelings were true, and I was in so much pain that naturally, I didn't want her to exist," I explained. This was one of the few times that I validated and honored my feelings and didn't fill my head and heart with guilt for what I experienced in the past.

My mom was not a nice person during this time, and my reaction to her was simply coming from a place of agony, torment, and hopelessness. I remember even during the times in which I was with my friends and my mom would do something else to upset me, I would say out loud, "I hate this woman," and my friends would say to me, "No, you don't hate her. That's your mom." I would, again, look at them directly in their eyes and say, "I don't care that she's my mom. I hate her!"

When they would ask about specifics as to why I felt like this towards her, I would just shrug it off and change the conversation. I was in hell but thought that this was what life was supposed to look and feel like. I also didn't know how to put into words what I was experiencing. Even now, I still struggle to put it into words or make sense of it. That and my mom had made it crystal clear that my brothers and I were not to discuss any of the household problems outside. She utilized fear as a tactic to make us believe that bad things would happen if we said anything to anyone and that it could even cause Child Protective Services to take us away from her. We were in hell but didn't want strangers to take us away from her. So, I remained silent with my friends, with social workers, with my family, and with teachers in school. To the world, everything was "normal."

It is ironic because, with the same intensity that I hated my mom, I also loved her. Months after she passed away, I found myself in a therapy session, but this time, it was not my session; it was my younger brother's session. At the time, he was struggling with expressing his anger, and my dad insisted that he had to accept going to counseling. Raylin obliged and attended a few sessions, but he didn't want to open up to the therapist. The therapist was out of ideas on how to get him to speak about what he was experiencing, so she asked for me to do a collateral session with him, where I could perhaps provide her with some insight. I agreed, and within the first ten minutes of the session, the therapist said to us, in an awful attempt to display "empathy," "You guys should have never been raised by your mother. You guys should have been removed from that household."

I remember looking at Raylin's face, and then, as I became filled with rage, I looked at her and said, "How dare you say that about our mother? Our mother was a great fucking mother, and you have no business in making that kind of remark, especially now that she is dead!"

I told Raylin to get up because we were leaving. Before exiting the office, I turned around and said, "You know something? If today you presented me with a lineup of ten potential mothers and asked me to choose a mom, I would pick my mom every single time."

We left, and I told Raylin that he didn't have to return to see that therapist ever again. I felt angry and hurt that my brother, while he was trying to grieve and make sense of life, had to listen to this woman's idiocy. I am sure she meant well, but these are the kind of comments that, as a therapist, you need to assess how beneficial it will be to the client as well as wait to build some kind of rapport. These are some of the fundamentals we learn in school as mental health counselors.

Even after my mother's death, I still felt responsible for protecting her. I protected her when she was alive, and I didn't see why that had to ever change. I knew who my mom was and all of the struggles she experienced. Our relationship was complicated. We loved each other. We hated each other. But she would always be my mother no matter what. I wasn't going to allow anyone to judge her.

My mom did the best she could at the time, and it has taken me years to acknowledge that truth. We all have coping mechanisms and build tough exteriors because of difficult experiences, fear, and insecurities. That is okay. What I have come to understand is that in the same way we built and learned to experience the world through these mechanisms, we can also put them down when we are ready to be vulnerable and tell our story because there is power in all of our stories.

Chapter 6

CARROT CAKE

If you asked eight-year-old me what I thought about carrot cake, I would probably make a disgusted face and tell you that it sounded gross. The thought of any vegetables mixed in a cake just seemed out of this world and even unnatural. Perhaps you are thinking by now, *Why on earth am I talking about carrot cake?!* Trust me, THERE IS A REASON TO MY MADNESS! At least, that is what I tell myself.

[Lighten up! Not everything that I have written in this book is intended to be heavy. You are permitted to laugh every few chapters... did you laugh yet? Great! Now I can continue.]

Today, when I think, see, smell, or even eat a piece of carrot cake, I think of my father. I instantly feel connected to him, and something as simple as a piece of cake transports me to a time when his love and support were always enough, no matter the circumstances. It was shortly after my parents' divorce that things started to get really ugly. And when I say ugly, I mean UGLY!

Part of the ugliness included my mother impulsively acting out against my dad in order to continually hurt him as much as she was hurting inside. That's the funny thing about "revenge" or trying to "get back" at someone; there is never a true end to the desired satisfaction that you are seeking in hurting others. I feel nothing but sadness when I think back on all the times that my mom tried to poison my mind against my father by saying hurtful things about him, things that I knew in my heart were not true. I feel sad that my mom felt so alone and powerless within herself that the only way she could try to ensure that my brothers and I would be on her side was to try to manipulate stories and make my dad seem like a big bad wolf. I didn't need to hear my dad's side or even ask him if half of the things she said were true because I just knew in my heart that who she was describing was not my dad.

My dad is kind, compassionate, and selfless. He doesn't mind working 14-hour days to provide for his family, and I can talk to him about anything without fear of judgment. He is someone who would take the food off his plate to give to someone else. He is everything and more than I could have ever asked for in a father. Most importantly, he is someone who tries to see the best in people, even during their difficult times. My dad has loved my brothers and me unconditionally, even during times when I didn't feel worthy of being loved. He is my best friend, and I am eternally grateful to be able to call him mine.

As I stated previously, my parents' divorce went from ugly to uglier, and between the times that my dad was arrested for accusations that my mom had manufactured and the times in which she would encourage my brothers and me to have a good relationship with my dad, I was sure to lose my mind. I wasn't sure what to make of all the mixed messages that I was receiving from her. On the one hand, it seemed as though she wanted us to hate him, and on the other hand, she wanted us to love him. We just couldn't love him more than her. She wanted to be the one we loved the most. She wanted to be the one that we would love unconditionally regardless of what she did or said. Trying to decipher all these messages felt like a never-ending puzzle, where pieces kept being added on. I danced on the ledge of insanity several times because just when I thought that I had figured it out, my mom would once again throw yet another curveball. If I did X, she would demand Y. If I then did Y, she would demand X.

My mom's curveballs came in different shapes and forms. At times, they came in increments, and at other times, they would be less subtle. It felt like I was on an episode of Jekyll and Hyde, and for some reason, the seasons kept getting renewed.

My mom had a sense of competition with my dad. Who was the better parent? Which parent was more loved? Which parent did more for their children? This was a rat race that seemed to have no beginning or end. It simply spiraled, sometimes more out of control than others, but nonetheless, it continued to spiral. There were times in which I felt so helpless and hopeless that my mother's attacks on my dad would never end that I wished he would just go away and not come back. Seeing and living through the hurt that my dad experienced hurt me that much more.

I was lost, stressed, anxious, worried, hypervigilant, and literally felt my stomach eating itself away from all of these emotions. That's the funny thing about emotions. It's not sufficient to feel them just mentally because they can also manifest themselves in physical form, like "Hello there, dear friend. Remember me? How about I make your stomach feel as though it's going to rip apart while producing a sensation that makes it feel that it's about to catch fire at the same time?" Sounds painful enough? I am here to tell you that it is. I noticed that even during my adulthood, whenever I felt stressed or had any unpleasant emotions, they would normally be accompanied by good ol' stomach pains. It got to the point where I developed gastritis, and doctors grew concerned that it would eventually escalate to an ulcer. Our emotions have a way of catching up with us when we try to avoid or silence them.

One of the not-so-pleasant experiences that my brothers and I had to live through was seeing my dad once a week during a supervised visit with a social worker, which was thanks to the restraining order that my mom had filed against him. Eventually, and over time, the judge showed some leniency with the restraining orders and granted my dad supervised visitation. This was a major blow for my dad, my brothers and me. To go from having the freedom of growing up with him and seeing him every day to now being limited to a miserable one-time-per-week visit and having a stranger in the room watching as if we were some kind of science experiment. It was difficult for me to digest, but I preferred to see him this way rather than not seeing him at all.

Initially, my brothers and I would go together on the train, and the journey would take us approximately 45 minutes. We would go inside the courthouse and into an office area, where my dad and a social worker were waiting for us to arrive. I felt so happy during these times and hugged my dad as soon as I saw him. The visits weren't long, and it was always hard having to say goodbye. I wanted nothing more than to go home with my dad. I wasn't even sure where my dad was living during this time. He didn't tell us out of fear of having my mom find out. My mom's actions became unpredictable, and my dad didn't want to take any more chances.

I wanted my dad to smile from the heart again. Even when he would smile, I could see the pain in his eyes. We tried to act normal, as if someone wasn't watching us, but I couldn't help but look at the social worker while she took notes on her notepad. I wondered how she was interpreting the information from our visit. Was she writing anything that would get my dad into trouble again? We tried to work around it by speaking in Spanish at times and hoped she didn't understand, but my dad would switch back to English because he didn't want to give the social worker the impression that he was saying anything negative.

Eventually, the visits became part of our routine. After school, my brothers and I took the train, saw my dad for a couple of hours, and then headed back home. There came a point at which Raymie stopped attending the visits. There were times he had school-related and sports-related activities, and there were other times in which he simply didn't want to go. Still, I continued going with Raylin. My birthday rolled around, and I was happy because I was able to see my dad. I knew it wouldn't be a celebration, but I at least got to spend time with him. As Raylin and I arrived at the office, my dad got up, hugged me, and wished me a happy birthday. The social worker's eyes lit up, and she asked, "Is it your birthday today?" and I said yes. She then looked at my dad and said, "Listen, I know you want to probably have some time with your daughter for her birthday. Why don't we have today's visit at the McDonald's nearby?" My dad agreed immediately, and I felt such an immense amount of happiness because, at least for that day, I didn't have to see my dad in this dull, dreadful office. Finally, someone else could see the good in my dad! With all of the previous court hearings, I couldn't understand why everyone seemed to blindly believe my mom but never really wanted to take into consideration my dad's side of the story.

We arrived at McDonald's, and the social worker told my dad that she knew he was a good guy and that she would give us some privacy. As we looked for a table, she pointed towards the area where she would be sitting and allowed us to sit at a table by ourselves. My dad had a bakery box with a cake inside, and I didn't know what kind it was until he opened it. Can you guess what cake it was? If you guessed carrot cake, then you are spot on!

My dad placed a candle on the cake, and he and Raylin sang Happy Birthday to me. I made a wish, and I still remember that wish. I wished that my mom would stop doing bad things to my dad so that my dad could be happy again. Without even thinking twice, I bit into the slice of cake and was surprisingly impressed! I loved the raisins and the flavors it had. It was not as gross or disgusting as I had previously thought. And even if it were gross, I would not have cared because this was coming from my dad. I thanked him for the cake and told him how much I loved it, especially after trying it for the first time. He turned to me and said, "Whenever you eat a piece of carrot cake again, you'll think of me and how much I love you no matter what. I love you guys to infinity and beyond." [Side note: we were fans of the movie *Toy Story*, so we tailored the phrase "to infinity and beyond" to "I love you to infinity and beyond." That's my dad for you. I love him with every fiber of my soul.]

Shortly after, the social worker alerted us that our visit for the day was done, and we thanked her so many times for the humanity that she showed us that day. She could have not cared. She could have done so many things that were a part of her job. Instead, she chose to be human first and then a social worker, and for that, I am eternally grateful.

If you asked me today what my favorite cake is, I would tell you it is carrot cake. Because when we had nothing else, we had each other. And we had carrot cake!

Chapter 7

OUTRUNNING THE DARKNESS

Have you ever experienced a time when you felt that with each difficult experience, you became more exhausted? The kind of exhaustion that sleep couldn't cure? It is the kind of exhaustion that comes from the soul, where you just feel tired of feeling the way you have been for what feels like a lifetime. And for some reason, it seems that our only way out of that state of exhaustion and pain is by not being here. Not being in this world.

In my experience, it has been quite common for people to start feeling uneasy anytime I would say things like this. The minute they saw the direction that the conversation was going, I could almost immediately sense their discomfort and urge to want to get out of the conversation. The sad part was that a lot of times, because of their discomfort, I silenced a lot of these thoughts and feelings. In turn, I felt my soul even more depleted and exhausted than ever.

We aren't usually taught how to sit with conversations about the realness of life. We think that our job is to think positively and to feel happy when, in reality, that is just one fragment of life. Is it not normal to feel sad? Is it not normal to not feel like life is a blessing and gift every single day? This kind of ideology and established norm is what pushed me so many times to feel like I was alone. I couldn't talk about how I was truly feeling or what my experience looked like because it wasn't acceptable. There was something that I must have been doing wrong to experience these kinds of thoughts.

It seemed like the cure to my unhappiness and exhaustion was to counter these thoughts and feelings with superficial positive thoughts and fake happiness. I was told to be grateful when I was living in my own hell. I was told to think positively when I saw nothing but darkness. I was told to live on when I felt dead inside. I am sure everyone meant well, but sometimes meaning well just isn't enough. It wasn't enough on the days that I felt like my existence was consuming me. These thoughts and feelings have haunted me for years, and they still haunt me today. These must have been the same thoughts and feelings that haunted my mother as well because when she was alive, I couldn't understand why she didn't want to exist.

As I reflect on my mom's inner turmoil, I am reminded of my own hell. I now see her experience with a level of understanding and compassion that I didn't have at the time with her. As a kid, watching her struggle and listening to her talk about how alone and abandoned she felt, I couldn't understand how she could feel all these things if she had my brothers and me. We were with her physically; we cared for her, so why couldn't this be enough?

Our first trip after my parents got divorced was to Disney World in Florida. I was 11 years old at the time, and as much as I wanted to look forward to this trip, it just didn't feel right. So much had happened in the months preceding the divorce that I had no idea how my mom would act during the trip. Would she be normal? Would we be able to enjoy it? A part of me wished my dad would have joined us as well because, at least then, I knew everything would have been okay.

My mom had already started to pack a few days before the trip. For a moment, I felt optimistic that my mom's troubling phase had finally passed. She seemed calm, although quieter than usual. She spent more time in her room with the door closed. I wasn't sure what was going on with her, but I figured that having her in this state was better than having her bounce off the walls.

One day, my brothers and I were watching TV in the living room while my grandma was cooking in the kitchen. My mom walked towards the kitchen, and I couldn't see what she was doing, but I heard a shuffling of the utensils in the drawer. I thought that perhaps she was hungry and was making herself something to eat, but then I noticed that she had put something inside her pajamas as she rushed out of the kitchen. I had no clue what was happening, but my heart began to race. I stood up and tried to talk to her in an attempt to stall her. Stall her from what? I had no idea, but I felt in my chest and gut that something was off about her. My stalling attempts were short-lived, and she rushed past me and locked herself in the bathroom.

I began to scramble. I went into the kitchen and told my grandma that something was going on with my mom. When she asked me to explain what was happening, I told her that I didn't know but that I had a feeling she was going to try to kill herself. The moment the words flew out of my mouth, I ran and banged on the bathroom door. As my mom opened the door, I saw her sitting on the floor, crying, with bloodied wrists and a kitchen knife on the floor. Instead of panicking, I got on my knees and told my mom she would be okay. I grabbed the first towel I could find and wrapped her wrists with it. I then helped her get off the floor and walked her to her bed. I called for Raymie and my grandma to help me. When they got to the room, the first thing they asked was, "What happened?" Everyone was in shock, but by this time, I was in go mode!

I told them to stay with my mom and add pressure to her wrists to keep her from bleeding out. I searched the bathroom cabinets for gauze but couldn't find any. So, I grabbed Raylin and went to the pharmacy to buy some supplies. My instinct was to take Raylin with me because he was the youngest, and I didn't want him to see what was going on.

We ran back, and I disinfected my mom's wrists with rubbing alcohol and then wrapped them with gauze. I gave her Tylenol for the pain and put her to bed. By this time, she seemed more calm and tired. I turned off the lights and closed her bedroom door so that she could rest. My brothers and I didn't say much about what had just happened. I had this heart-sinking feeling that this would only be the first of many attempts. It seemed that our hell had taken another kind of turn. The pain that my mom was once projecting outwards was now being projected against herself. I didn't know how I would deal with the situations to come, but I was simply relieved that we were able to get to her in time for this one.

I look back on this experience with mixed feelings. The combination of my experiences and trauma has taught me to be hypervigilant and observant, which has served me a great deal during questionable situations. But the combination of my experiences and trauma has also robbed me of my innocence. It has robbed me of being able to be fully present in the moment because my body has already been conditioned to be hyper-aware and expect the unexpected. My sensory system has been on overdrive for as long as I can remember, and fun can sometimes feel exhausting because if I am having fun, who is paying attention to all the possibilities? This, my friends, is how you exhaust yourself until what feels like the point of no return. The accumulation of worry and stress, the need to be in control, and always being the one to fix it all will do quite a number on your mind, body, spirit, and soul.

After my mom's suicide attempt, I didn't know if we would still be able to go on our Disney trip. Quite frankly, I was hoping my mom would just cancel it because going to a new environment would simply add another element to the chaos. To my surprise, my mom continued with the plans for the trip, and we went on our Disney vacation.

I wanted to be excited about the trip, but there was a huge part of me that wouldn't allow me to be. I had to pay close attention to my mother's movements and actions in case something else happened. I followed her like a shadow because at least if she was in sight, I could assess whether she needed help or if she was fine. I was far from happy. We went to a couple of the parks, and she really tried to show us a good time, but she couldn't hide the fact that she wasn't feeling physically or mentally well. All I remember from being at Disney, the supposed happiest place on earth, was feeling very hot. We had to wait in long lines to get on any of the rides, and all of the stores looked like a can of sardines from all the crowds of people. I saw kids laughing and parents playing with their kids, yet here we were, trying to pretend we were like them.

I was not a fan of Disney World, but my brothers and I had a blast in the hotel pool. This was one of the few times when I felt like I could be a kid. We goofed around and played for hours until it was time to go back to our room. My mom tried to join us in our fun, but we still saw that she wasn't fully present.

I have to give my mom so much credit because, despite everything that happened and the turmoil she was experiencing, she was still trying to be our mother. She was trying to provide us with what she thought would make us happy. The one thing that would've made me happy during that trip was to see her happy and no longer in pain.

The months went by, and as I previously suspected, my mom had reoccurring suicide attempts. Time after time, I observed her patterns and her possible triggers. I noticed that whenever conversations with her would turn into conflict or she felt like she wasn't being heard, it would usually take her to the dark mental space of not wanting to be alive. This became almost part of our routine. I would try to de-escalate situations before she got to the point of wanting to harm herself, but usually, my attempts were in vain. I then started to hide the kitchen knives, and when she realized what I was doing, she would try to convince me to give them to her by saying that she needed to cut something in the kitchen. I fell for her trick once and gave her one of the knives. Before I knew it, she ran with it straight to the bathroom. That was the last time I gave in. After she realized that I wouldn't budge on giving her knives, she tried to wait for my grandma to cook and would persuade her to give her a knife. I caught on immediately, and anytime I saw her heading towards the kitchen, I would stand by the door watching. One time, she looked at me and asked, "Are you okay? Why are you always following me?" I couldn't believe she was asking *me* this after all of the back and forth we had been doing for months.

Besides trying to thwart her multiple suicide attempts, there were scheduled court visits and appointments I had to attend due to the ongoing chaos surrounding my parents' divorce. Some of these appointments included scheduled home visits as part of the custody hearing. During these visits, a social worker would come and ask routine questions. She had to ensure that my mom was a competent mother and that we were living in safe conditions. I remember right before one particular visit, my mom gathered my brothers and me in the living room. She told us that we couldn't tell the social worker about anything that had happened in our home, including why she had bandages on her wrists. She told us that if the social worker found out about her suicide attempts, we would be taken from our home and placed into foster care. I knew that what we were experiencing at home was tough, but at least it was with our mom and not a stranger. There was not a hell worse than the hell we didn't know.

One time, the social worker arrived and did her routine check. During her routine questioning, she happened to look at my mother's wrapped wrists. "What happened to your wrists, Mrs. Yturrino?" As the last word left the social worker's mouth, I literally stopped breathing. I didn't know what lie my mom could've come up with that would've been believable.

Without hesitation, my mom told her that she had accidentally burned herself with the toaster oven. By the expression on the social worker's face, I knew that she didn't buy what my mom was selling. I literally thought, *Crap! She knows Mom is lying*. The social worker raised her eyebrows. "How is it possible that you burned *both* of your wrists with the toaster oven?" Casually and expertly, my mom lied. "The kids were horsing around in the kitchen and knocked over the toaster oven. And before it fell on the floor, I caught it with my arms."

As I witnessed the lie leave my mom's lips, all I could think was, *Well played, Mom! When in doubt, blame the kids!*

[Okay, if you didn't laugh there, then my friend, you might want to lighten up a little. It's not meant to be all serious. Trust me.]

I look back on this now and laugh with my brothers because there wasn't a situation my mom couldn't bullshit her way out of. The kinds of stories she came up with were enough to create a soap opera. She was witty and astute. You could not catch her slipping.

I am not sure what went through the mind of the social worker, but she accepted my mom's story. She eventually left, and I felt relieved that she hadn't taken us away. In my view, this was a win because now that someone on the outside had noticed my mom's wrists, I hoped that it would deter her from continuing with her suicide attempts. Having people notice what was actually happening at home was something she didn't want, so I thought it would finally all stop. Right? WRONG!

Instead of cutting her wrists, she upgraded to trying to overdose on her prescribed medications. She had a whole pharmacy of medication that she took on a daily basis because, after every doctor's appointment, she seemed to always come back home with more. I found it interesting how doctors never seemed to reduce any of her medications. Instead, they would just sell her by saying, "There's this new medication on the market that has worked for patients like you." And, of course, my mom bought into it every time because, at the end of the day, she just wanted to get better. She wanted to finally feel normal.

The first few times she tried to overdose on medications, I only realized that something was off when my brothers and I noticed that she hadn't woken up all day. Granted, my mom was a deep sleeper, but during these instances of her overdosing, there was just no waking her up. Often, her medication bottles would have the lid off, which was an indicator that she had probably taken more than she should have. We called 911, and every time EMS asked what had happened, I was nervous about telling them that she had tried to overdose on her medication. I knew that there would be repercussions, but I knew if I didn't tell them, there would be a chance that they wouldn't be able to help her. There were several times when she was transferred to the psychiatric unit of the hospital, and there were other times when doctors believed her when she told them she had overdosed "accidentally." She would either tell them that she was in so much pain that she decided to take more of her medication in hopes that she would get some relief, or she would blame it on her memory and tell them that she simply had forgotten that she had taken her medication already. When she returned home, I tried to use the same strategy that I previously used with the kitchen knives, but the problem was that she actually needed her medication, so hiding them wouldn't work. I tried to supervise her while she took her medications, but any time she took more than what the label indicated, she would shrug it off and tell me that the dosage had changed.

Eventually, this became the norm as well. Doesn't everyone's mother try to kill themselves at least ten times per month? No? Just mine? Okay, perhaps my humor has become too dark. Truth is, over time, I became desensitized. There was so much that I was feeling and living through that I just accepted that this is what life looked like for us. As long as no one on the outside found out, everything would continue to work out some way, somehow.

One particular night, my mom woke me up at around 2:00 a.m. and told me to get out of bed. I followed her to the bathroom, and she started to cry and told me that she had overdosed on her medication again. I looked at her and felt exhausted. How much more could I take of this? By this time, I was an expert on helping her induce her own vomiting because it seemed to be the only way to get the medication out of her system. So, I told her to do the same as she had done the previous times. I didn't feel scared. I didn't feel nervous. I just felt exhausted and annoyed. But at that moment, I knew I had to do something.

"Did you try to vomit already?" I asked.

"Yes, but nothing is coming out," she sobbed, scared.

"Do you want me to call the ambulance then?"

"No! I don't want to get admitted again to the psychiatric ward," she cried.

I became annoyed.

"You know you wouldn't have to worry about this if you just stopped trying to overdose and kill yourself! You want to kill yourself but also want me to help you not die," I replied angrily.

I knew I was being cruel and hurting her, but I just didn't have the capacity to care. She was creating this problem, and every single time, I had to be the one to save her. She looked at me and continued to cry. I then called 311, which is the information hotline in NY, and asked them "hypothetically" about what someone should do if they accidentally overdosed on medication. I assured them it wasn't about me and that it was just for a friend who didn't know what to do. Like my mom, I also became astute and quick to cover up what was going on with her.

Eventually, after several attempts, my mom was finally able to vomit out her medication. Tired, both figuratively and literally, I put her to bed. As I made my way back to my room, I could only wonder when this nightmare would be over. I no longer felt sorry for her. I felt angry towards her for everything she was putting my brothers and me through. This wasn't fair!

One of the last times she had overdosed on her medications, I remember walking in on her as she was chugging down an entire bottle filled with pills. I felt so numb at this moment, and all I could say was, "Here we go again."

Everything had been revolving around her and making sure that she was okay. My brothers and I were literally living in hell, and it felt as though she and the world could give two flying shits. Everything was about her. Even though people tried to help, it felt like it wasn't enough. Could they not see beyond the silence and the lies we were forced to tell? Every time someone reached out to help, I internally hoped that this person would finally be the one to save us from all of this. Someone that could help her return to being the mom she once was. But at the time, it felt like that person didn't exist, so we would have to continue doing this on our own.

I didn't try to stop her this time; I simply grabbed the phone and called 911. I didn't even ask her if she was okay. The operator quickly answered. "911, What's your emergency?" Unemotional, I responded. "My mom is overdosing. She is right in front of me, chugging down her medications." As my mom and I waited for the ambulance to arrive, I looked at her and encouraged her to continue taking all of her medications. "Don't you want to die? Continue taking it then." At that moment, I didn't care about anything. I was drained. We had already been through this so many times before, and there seemed to be no end in sight.

The ambulance finally arrived and took her to the hospital. When she left, I thought to myself, *I hope she doesn't come back for a long time because then I wouldn't have to watch her or worry about the next time.*

In between this reality, my brothers and I tried to pretend like everything was fine on the outside. We rarely missed a day of school, and everything was fine as long as we didn't think or talk about our lives at home. The routine question, "How are you?" was abruptly answered with the auto-response, "I'm fine." That's what my life was like for a long time. To the world, I was just fine.

My brothers and I also used humor... a LOT of it to cope with life at home. There would be times when, before opening the front door, we would look at each other and sarcastically say, "I wonder what hell awaits us today." From the front door, we could see whether our mom's bedroom door was open or closed. When we saw that it was closed, we would sigh with relief and jokingly say, "Thank God the beast is asleep." Other times, when she was awake, there was not much talking between any of us. "Hello" was sometimes the most interaction we would have because it felt safer to say little or nothing at all. We were all drained and trying to just get through the day. Through it all, I am so grateful to have had my brothers by my side. I am not sure how I could've made it through everything without them and their morbid yet hysterical sense of humor. There were a lot of tears, but there was also a lot of laughter because we had each other.

Why was this my mom? Why couldn't she stop doing these things? What was so wrong with her life that she kept running towards death? How could she want to die if she had to take care of us even though we were caring more for her?

I didn't understand any of this until I found myself in a similar state of mind. Experience has been one hell of a teacher in my life. It wasn't until my mom passed away that I felt and experienced the desolation that she so often talked about. I remember all of the times that she would tell me how, in a room full of people, she still felt so alone. I didn't understand this because I thought that being around people made us feel less alone. But it's not always that simple. My mom struggled with many demons in her life, and I think one of her biggest demons was feeling detached from the world. She tried and tried, but for some reason, she still managed to feel this pain. No matter how much she fought, the pain and suffering never seemed to leave her. All this time, I had thought that my mom was running towards death or seeking attention when, in reality, all she wanted was to not feel her pain anymore. She didn't actually want to die. She was just exhausted from her reality and didn't see another way out. How many of us haven't experienced this?

I know I have experienced this feeling many times feeling like I wasn't enough. I have felt disconnected from people, places, and experiences. I have felt this cloud of pain and sadness follow me no matter how far I have tried to run from it or cover it up. I haven't been able to think it away or pretend it doesn't exist. We inherit and learn many things from our parents, including our perception of the world. After she passed away, I was able to see and experience some of what tormented her because it also tormented me. I tried to resist and reject becoming like my mother because I refused to be like her. The more I resisted, the more I suffered and the more stuck I felt. In my own resistance to becoming my mother, I unconsciously was denying my experience with her. There was just no way that there wouldn't be any collateral damage from all that we experienced together.

We were all a part of it.

On days when the dark cloud feels heavier and bigger, I remind myself how much worse I felt when I tried to run from it. I have learned to show myself more grace and allow myself to lean into the heaviness when it surfaces. When I was experiencing everything with my mom, I didn't have the capacity to process my reactions and emotions that came with it. I was in survival mode and couldn't afford to feel what came up at the moment. The accumulation of all these experiences will take time to process, and that is okay. I don't always get it right, but I have tried to release the urgency and pressure of time in order to honor my experience and the ever-changing seasons of my life.

Life is not always going to feel and look bright, and this is okay! We are not less of a human being just because we struggle. We are not less of a human being just because we don't feel happy and think positively all the time. It is when we treat and honor all of our reactions and emotions equally that we truly understand that this is all part of our human experience. Healing, I've learned, is a journey. And healing doesn't mean that we no longer struggle with our past. Rather, healing is being able to sit and cope with our emotions and experiences with compassion and understanding that no particular moment lasts forever.

And to my beautiful mother, I am sorry that you felt so alone during this time. I didn't understand how you could feel alone and still have us with you. I am sorry that no one heard and understood you. If you were here right now, I would hug you tightly and tell you that I get it now. I now understand that you tried your best even when it felt like your worst. I love you yesterday, today, and forever.

Chapter 8

LONELINESS – OUR GREATEST CONNECTION

This chapter, by far, has been the most uncomfortable to write, and I have put it down more times than I have picked it up. I was doing well with the previous chapters I had written and felt like I was finally in the "flow" of things until I wasn't. Currently, though, I am writing this chapter on a beautiful island in Hong Kong called Lantau Island. It is nighttime, and as I sit by the ocean, the sound of the waves helps me feel at home within myself. I relocated to Hong Kong in the hopes of finding Lindsay and who she is outside of everything and everyone familiar. I know what you are probably thinking: this is a far way from home to simply go looking for yourself! I agree, but I've learned to be open to life experiences and allow myself to be led to the places and experiences that I would have never previously imagined. I truly believe that it is through our experiences, both pleasant and unpleasant, that we truly are able to look deep within ourselves and understand ourselves that much better.

Loneliness was a term that I didn't always understand but somehow felt. It was as though it had been ingrained into my soul and my essence. It followed me through the day and slept with me through the night. The only way I could describe my experience prior to finding a label or word for it was the sense of feeling separate from those around me. There was me, and then there were people. I saw people laugh, and I laughed. I saw people speak, so I spoke. I saw people have fun, so I had fun. But when it was all over, and it was time to go back home, I felt this heavy weight of sadness overcome my body. It was this dark energy that flowed through my veins, and it magnified its intensity once it knew that I was alone. For some time, and even up until recently, I described it as a dark cloud that seemed to follow me no matter what. It made me believe that happiness was just simply not in the cards for me because no matter what happened externally or internally, I still felt the same: empty. Where was this emptiness coming from, and why could I never seem to fill the void?

It wasn't until approximately one week prior to my relocating to Hong Kong that I started to understand my loneliness from a different perspective. I signed up for a virtual guided meditation with an amazing human being who works with people to heal their "mother wound." (I strongly encourage you to research the mother wound and the powerful impact that the mother wound has on our lives.) I went through the guided meditation, and when the session started, we talked about my loneliness. I explained to her that my current relationship had ended, and I was moving to another country on my own. I felt that I needed to start to listen to my loneliness before it started to consume my existence, as it had already done so many times before.

I explained that I had dealt with many painful experiences and used that harbored pain to help me navigate life. When life had become a bit complicated, or things hadn't gone how I envisioned or wanted them to, I tended to resort to what felt natural to me. At the age of 29, I understood that while pain, depression, and loneliness were all places I used to live, they no longer were places that I had to continue residing. I was choosing to go back to those places because, for so many years, I knew pain, depression, and loneliness as my home, so it was natural for me to think that they would continue to be my home. After several different conversations with people who have come into my life as angels with messages, I understood that I was the only one who could break free from the places that I had known as home but no longer needed to live in.

During my virtual meditation, I was mentally brought into a place where I visualized my loneliness as a black rock, and in front of me was my mother. This meditation brought up a lot of mixed feelings for me because a big part of me yearned to wake up and see my mother, and the other part of me felt this immense pain and weight from the black rock. There we were all together: me, the rock, and my mom. I was given a choice to hand over the black rock that represented my loneliness to my mother or to keep it to myself. As I extended my hand to give her the rock, I took it back and decided to keep it as I did not want her to carry pain, even in death. The decision to remain with my loneliness brought out tears and pain that flowed out of me like it had not done so before. I cried because, as much as I didn't want to feel this way, I also didn't want to burden my mom.

This exercise and my ultimate decision to stay with the rock were symbolic of our relationship. When she was alive, no matter what she did and how it made me feel, there was a need for me to see and make her happy or, at least, to make her feel better. I couldn't see my mother in pain, even when I was in pain. From a young age, because I had learned to navigate through this world of depression, pain, and loneliness, I preferred to internalize and absorb the unpleasant emotions from situations rather than have my mom, dad, and brothers experience those emotions. Seeing them in pain caused me greater pain. And still, to this day, it causes me a great deal of pain and distress when I know that my dad and/or brothers are struggling.

After the meditation was over, I was able to speak to the guide about the meditation, where she provided some insight. She explained that I didn't give back my loneliness to my mother because it was the way we connected. We learned how to connect through pain and feelings of not being enough for one another, so when I felt lonely, depressed, or in pain, I was consciously and unconsciously connecting with my mother. To let go of that rock would have meant for me, at that point, to let go of my mother. Damn! As I heard these simple yet powerful words, I felt like the veil had literally been lifted from my face. I felt like, for the first time in my life, I saw my loneliness for what it was rather than something that followed me like a shadow. I realized that a lot of the reason why I held onto this loneliness, depression, and pain was because I didn't know how else to connect with my mother.

My experiences with my mom taught me to expect the unexpected. It taught me to not be too happy because those moments would be short-lived. My experiences taught me to be hypervigilant and not say too much in front of my mom because it may have caused a reaction. And even when there was nothing particularly going on, I saw and absorbed her sadness, her pain, her loneliness. My mom would often tell me that in a room full of people, she felt this deep sense of loneliness. And at the time, I didn't understand. I was doing everything in my power to be there for her and to be everything she needed, and in trying to be everything for my mom, I became nothing for myself. Her death left me feeling like nothing and as though I had no one else to be everything for.

My meditation session ended, and I felt like I finally saw life very differently at this point. It was the reset and understanding that I needed before embarking on my new life in Hong Kong. Little did I know what waited for me ahead.

The COVID-19 Pandemic hit and impacted life as we all knew it. That included travel restrictions around the world, and my journey to Hong Kong would be everything but simple. Prior to my trip, I had to get tested and have my results back 72 hours prior to my flight. While it was a mission to accomplish, I was able to get the results on the same day of my flight. I was relieved, nervous, and excited to start my new life in Hong Kong. While I didn't know what was ahead, I was ready for the adventure and to experience life in a different country. Saying goodbye to my dad, stepmom, brother, and sister at the airport was bittersweet. I was sad because I wasn't sure when the next time I would see them would be because of the travel restrictions, but I was happy about finally being able to leave.

Everything seemed to be going smoothly up until I landed at my connecting destination, Los Angeles. I will save you some time and let you know that I was not able to board my flight to Hong Kong in L.A. because I was told that the COVID-19 test had to have been done 72 hours prior to my connecting flight in L.A. and not the New York flight. I demanded to speak with a supervisor, as I had previously called several times to check on the COVID-19 policy. I explained the details of my situation, and her response remained the same, "Ma'am, unfortunately, you are unable to board this flight as your test results are not within the necessary timeframe."

For the first time in my life, my brain was not racing at 1,000 mph, creating solutions and alternatives. Instead, my mind went blank. I walked outside of the airport in the wee hours of the morning and simply stood outside with no plan. I couldn't think. I just stared at the cars driving by in disbelief. After a few minutes, my brain finally began to work, and I came to terms with the fact that I would need to get a hotel for the night and get info on testing centers first thing in the morning. I was relieved to have found an available hotel on my phone, so I booked it and was on my way.

Los Angeles, from what I saw on TV and in the movies, seemed to be an amazing place. One filled with glitz, glamor, and celebrities (Hello, Hollywood!). So I was surprised by what I saw when I pulled up to the hotel. I felt as though I had walked into a dangerous neighborhood, and no one in the lobby area looked friendly AT ALL. I kept telling myself that it wasn't the fact that the hotel seemed "hood," as I would call it; it was the fact that there is no worse hood than the hood that you are not familiar with!

After five flights of stairs and no working elevator, I got to my room, and the bright red color of the bedding and carpet caused me to feel an overwhelming sense of stress and anxiety about what I was currently living through. The room didn't even look like it had been cleaned, and I was mortified that I would get sick just by being in that room. I sat on the corner of the bed and wailed uncontrollably. I cried and cried because never in my life had I felt so alone physically and emotionally. I was alone, in a state where I didn't know anyone, and it was the middle of the night. I was not confident that I would be able to make it to Hong Kong after all. For the first time, I felt like I couldn't pretend that I was okay. I closed my eyes for a total of 30 minutes and stayed awake until morning.

As soon as it was 6:00 a.m., I ordered a cab and waited in the lobby for it to arrive. I couldn't leave that awful hotel fast enough! During my wait, I spoke to my dad and brothers and told them about what was going on. The three of them were sorry that I was going through this difficulty but were also upset that I didn't call them when everything was initially happening. My first thought to their anger was, "What good would it have done for me to worry them in the middle of the night about this?! It's not like they would be able to do something for me from New York!" They asked me to keep them posted and let them know of my progress with the COVID-19 test and flight to Hong Kong. As my cab arrived, I sat in the back and was greeted by the nicest Hispanic cab driver.

"What are you doing staying in a hotel on this side of town?"

"I have no idea. I wasn't even supposed to be here this weekend. I was meant to be here just for a couple of hours for my connecting flight to Hong Kong."

"Well, it looks like life had other plans for you this weekend and insisted that you get to experience California before leaving the country," he replied, laughing.

He took me to the drive-through testing site that the airline had recommended. The airline supervisor told me that this site normally gave results back within a few hours, which would have allowed me to fly to Hong Kong that same day.

As I waited to get tested, I explained my situation to the clinic representative, and he gave me the *worst possible* news. "Your results won't be back until at least midnight the next day."

There had to be a mistake! The airport said that I'd get them back the same day! I tried to re-explain my situation in hopes that there was some sort of miscommunication. Unfortunately, he repeated what I already had heard: midnight the next day.

At this point, I didn't say anything or react. I was exhausted, and reacting or feeling would have cost me energy that I didn't have. I realized that I would have to stay in California for another day. I have learned that in life, things will happen as they are supposed to and not how we always want them to. I knew there was something for me to understand; I just didn't know what.

Luckily, the driver waited for me outside of the testing site. I got into the car and didn't say anything, but he knew that I felt defeated. I felt like everything that I had worked for up until this moment was collapsing right in front of me. The night before, I thought that I wouldn't make it to Hong Kong, but now I was sure. The driver looked at me and asked if I wanted to see the nicer part of Los Angeles while he drove by Santa Monica Beach. I had nothing but time at that point and agreed. On our drive there, I cleared out my mind somehow and was able to focus on the moment: on the pretty sky, on the wind blowing through my hair, on the sun, on the road, and on views of the water. I was there for that moment, and nothing else mattered. This driver will never know the life that he gave me during this time when I felt depleted and as though I had nothing else to give.

To that cab driver: If you are reading this, I want you to know that you were my angel during this time. You allowed me to see the beauty of life no matter how hard it got. For that, I will always be thankful.

As our tour ended, he asked where I wanted to go, and I told him that I would just wait for my results at the airport because I didn't want to return to that awful hotel. I was messaging my brothers at the same time and explained to them my plan. Raymie urged me to simply find another hotel and that he would cover the costs. I was going through the little money that I had saved for the trip on these unexpected hiccups, but even still, I insisted that I would pay for whatever hotel I found. I was not sure what was working inside of me, whether it was my need to show that I could take care of myself or the discomfort I felt in accepting that I needed help. Eventually, though, I gave in and accepted his help.

When I arrived at the second hotel, I was surprised to realize that I had booked a shared room. As I entered the door, I was greeted by a man who was also staying in the room. "Hi," he said. I was in disbelief. I received a text message from Raymie, who apparently saw the screenshot of the hotel details I had sent earlier in the day and told me to find a single room or another hotel immediately. By this point, I felt like giving up and going back home, but somehow, I continued.

I quickly gathered my belongings and headed down to the concierge to see if a single room was available. I received another text from Raymie, and it read, "How are you doing?" As I was typing my response, I started to cry and admitted to him that I was falling apart. I couldn't take it anymore. He sent me words of encouragement and told me that I was going to get through this.

Luckily, the hotel was able to accommodate my single-room request. When I made it to the room, I sat on the bed and cried for 40 minutes straight. It hit me at that point that I was not alone and, despite what I told myself throughout the years, I have never been alone. I know this is going to sound absurd, but after my mom passed away, I chose to be alone. I chose to be alone every time I rejected my family and friends' help. I chose to be alone when people asked how I was doing, and I lied through my teeth. "I'm fine." I chose to be alone, as I needed evidence to prove that I didn't need anyone or their help. I saw accepting help as being weak. I couldn't and wouldn't accept help because I wasn't a victim. I had figured life out on my own up until this point. Why should this time be any different?

Shortly after my meltdown, Raymie sent me more money to treat myself to lunch, and I was able to have a delicious burger from a restaurant downstairs. As I lay on the bed, I started receiving an overwhelming amount of support from my family and friends. I got back to the room, and each one of them sent me a message of encouragement and support. My Venmo account was ringing out of control because none of them wanted me to worry about finances during this time. The outpour of support that I was receiving made the reason for my journey in California crystal clear.

I felt like another layer of the veil was removed, and I finally felt open to receiving, which was something that had felt impossible before. I am blissfully grateful for having experienced this moment in my life. It was a difficult realization because I had to turn the mirror to myself to see myself for who I truly was. I understood that while pain, depression, and loneliness came as a result of my experiences, I also entertained and invited them into my life, time and time again. I have kept them in my life by pushing away any sign of help and, most importantly, by closing the door, not allowing people to see the real me. The real me would have to be vulnerable, raw, and open. I knew that this was only the beginning of finding myself, but what a way to start my new life and journey. I was able to leave for Hong Kong the next day and arrived safely.

I would be lying if I sat here and told you that I no longer feel depressed, in pain, or lonely. The ghosts of my past still visit me, but they no longer feel like an overwhelming burden. For a long time, I felt hopeless about being able to experience peace or happiness because the unpleasant emotions seemed to take up too much of my internal space. Now that I can finally allow myself to trust in my support system, I know that I don't have to face these emotions or experiences on my own. And this process has taught me how to make space for all of the emotions that live within all of us.

My loneliness my shadow you no longer follow me the same way. Instead, I now see you in front of me when you come to visit, where I hold you for the time you need and show you how much love you have from so many people in your life.

My loneliness my shadow I will no longer hide you or run from you. Instead, I will embrace you and be open to you showing me the different unhealed parts of myself that I have yet to meet.

My loneliness my shadow I thank you because I know I have a lot to learn, but I know you bring me closer to finding Lindsay again.

The version of me 15 years ago experienced loneliness very differently. I experienced loneliness as a curse; as something that I was born with. Prior to moving to Hong Kong, I believed no, I knew that my loneliness belonged to me. My loneliness symbolized how, throughout most of my challenging experiences, I've had to walk alone. I've had to "figure things out." I've had to push my feelings to the side in order to continue moving forward and overcoming the experiences that I was presented with. However, have I really overcome those experiences if the remnants of them seem to linger? They linger, and the more experiences I've had to work through and "figure out," the heavier I have felt. It is like the snowball effect, where every ounce of snow has added to this massive snowball. See, that's the price of resiliency. I have found that while there are purpose and positive aspects of resiliency that allow us to overcome adversity, it also comes with a price. Resiliency has cost me a lot. Being the "strong" one and the one that keeps going no matter what has cost me a lot. Because with resiliency, I haven't honored the emotions that come up with difficult experiences. To honor those emotions would have meant that I would have had to process that experience at that moment. And that would have most likely broken me down and not allowed me to continue pushing forward from one difficult experience to the next.

I experienced loneliness as this dark cloud that would follow me no matter how far I tried to run away from it. See, that, in itself, has been the problem all along. I have felt as though my loneliness was something to run from. I felt that I was lonely, and loneliness was me. I found myself trying to fill that loneliness with my romantic relationships. I expected my partners to love me the way I didn't know how to love myself. See, I believed for a long time that we could only receive love from the outside. I had no idea that it was possible to give love to ourselves.

I didn't think that I deserved grace. I didn't think that I deserved empathy. A part of my loneliness has come from how I tend to unconsciously (and consciously) keep people at a distance from me because I had convinced myself that I wasn't a victim and, therefore, didn't want anyone's pity. I learned that when you tell your story to people or when you open up about a difficult experience, people tend to feel sorry for you. And I didn't want anyone to feel sorry for me. I still don't want anyone to feel sorry for me. However, today, I don't want anyone to pity me because I am grateful for every beautiful, happy, loving, miserable, heart-wrenching, and every other kind of experience that I have ever had.

I have accumulated emotions and reactions from 20-plus years of experience, and yet I wonder where this loneliness has come from. Why does this loneliness follow me like a shadow? As I write this, I am having a conversation with myself and trying to allow myself to be open and honest, not just with you but also with myself. We want to think that we have it all figured out or that we are put together. That could not be farther from the truth. The difference between me today and me 15 years ago is that I try to show myself a bit more grace now. I try to remind myself that it is okay to fall apart and that it is okay to not have the strength to push forward. As I write those words, my eyes fill with tears because that message is a message that I have not allowed myself to receive before.

This is a mindset shift that has taken me many, many, MANY years to get to because, for a long time, I resented my difficult experiences. I looked at those difficult experiences as having done something to me and as having hurt me. And while yes, those experiences definitely hurt and caused me a great deal of pain, they have also molded me into the person that I am today. It has allowed me to see the different facets of myself. Because we are not just one individual; we are so many individuals in one. I know it sounds crazy, but it is the truth as I see and feel it. There is no simple way to describe ourselves or who we are. We are beings with so many layers, and the pleasant and unpleasant experiences peel back those layers. Some layers are much harder to peel back than others, but that is where I found the most growth. Through the experiences that I thought would kill me, I found that they allowed me to survive time and time again. Through the tears, the pain, the hurt, I have survived, and I continue to survive every single day.

Chapter 9

MY LIFE AFTER LOSS

Life after loss has been a completely different experience than life before loss. Over time, I realized that it is through death that we, as a people, can truly see and experience life's fragility. With death, we experience grief and loss. Death can also lead us to hold on tighter to those who are still physically present with us. With death, we experience the temporariness of life and understand that we are on a journey that has a final destination.

For a long time, I felt traumatized by my mother's death. During the first three months, I replayed the days leading up to her death over and over again. I did this religiously in hopes that I would find the flaw; in hopes that I would find what I did wrong; in hopes that I would find the scenario that would have resulted in an outcome where she didn't die. I tortured myself with these thoughts, and all I could feel was anger. I felt angry because I knew that regardless of how many times I replayed her death in my head, no matter how many times I replayed all of the possible scenarios and what could've changed her death, I was still left with the emptiness from realizing that it didn't matter. It didn't matter how much I thought about her death; it didn't matter how many flaws I found within the situation, within myself; the outcome would always remain the same. It was the complete loss of control and power that I struggled with the most: to acknowledge and accept that I no longer had control over what happened to my mother. For so many years, I was there every single time to save her from the world and from herself.

I was there to bear witness to her agony. I was there to bear witness to her internal and external struggle, but the ONE FUCKING DAY she needed me the most, I wasn't there. That was a sentiment, guilt, and thought that I carried with me for a long time. I carried these feelings so long that I can't remember when I was able to let that weight go. Have I let that weight go?

When my mother became physically and mentally sick, I took up the responsibility of caring for her. I cared for her, even before the age that I learned to take care of myself. This was when I learned to "figure things out." I learned that when I didn't know something, I had to research and seek the answers; thus, my "figuring out" of life commenced. This trait proved to be helpful in the aspect that I typically have aimed towards being proactive about situations and challenges, meaning when life has confronted me with a challenge or task, no matter how big or small, I have been able to simultaneously analyze it from several angles and perspectives before coming up with a variety of solutions that could help solve or process whatever was in front of me. HELLO ANXIETY! This has allowed me to process information from a solution-focused perspective and also explore the world in a different light. For instance, when I was a senior in high school, I had no idea about the financial aid program that I would have to apply for to be able to afford college. All I knew was that my friends talked about their parents applying for them, and therefore, this was not something my friends really had to worry about because it was being taken care of.

I was in the process of applying for college, but I knew that FASFA was yet another task that I would have to "figure out." I tried to ask my brother for assistance, but like me, he also had to "figure it out" and wasn't sure how he did at the time. I then researched FASFA, which led me to the website, and I started the application on my own. I asked my mom a few questions about her income tax history, but I remember feeling intimidated because while I was trying to "figure out" what I was applying for, I also hoped that I wasn't answering questions incorrectly that would negatively affect my mom or me. I remembered clicking the submit button and not really knowing what the outcome would be, but I hoped to dear God that the application would be processed correctly. I checked the status consistently to ensure that I didn't have to submit any additional information. This was just a brief example of how I observed, took notes, and took action in order to continue to move forward and not miss an opportunity.

After my parents divorced, I didn't feel that I was able to rely on them for guidance. From my perspective, they had bigger issues to deal with, and I didn't want to burden them with my questions and problems. This has also served a purpose during the times when my family or friends found themselves in situations where they were unsure of what to do. For the most part, I have always been able to provide them with an objective lens that has helped give them clarity and solutions. As useful and resourceful as this skill or trait has been, it also instilled a need to "figure things out" ALL of the time, and this, my friend, is exhausting! It truly is tiresome to operate like a machine that constantly needs to be seeking and doing. While being able to help those around me has been rewarding and satisfying, it has also depleted my energy many times. Feeling like I constantly have to be on for myself and those around me has made having "off" days nearly impossible, and thus, the frustration and fatigue set in. This is why boundaries are so important to have for your own sake and for the sake of those who love and care about you.

With this fine-tuned trait of being able to "figure out" situation after situation, regardless of whether it directly involved me or not, I couldn't wrap my head around not being able to have "figured out" my mother's last day; my mother's last breath. I saved my mom so many times before, but I couldn't figure out why and how she died. With every suicide attempt, I was there to figure it out. So many times, I was able to anticipate and help her through another suicidal attempt. But I didn't anticipate the day that she died.

For a long time, I couldn't understand why she had to die. I couldn't understand why I didn't see her death coming. I couldn't understand why I was and still am able to figure everything else out, but I couldn't figure out how to take back the hands of time and bring my mom back. This led me to feel like I had failed. I had failed at the one thing that meant something: keeping my mom alive.

I became angry with myself because I didn't call her that morning of April 6th, 2011. If I would have called her, I would have sensed something in her voice. If I would have called her, I would have known what to do. If I had called her, I would've "figured it out." But I didn't. And that's a reality that was hard for me to accept but one that I had to come to terms with in order to stop punishing myself. I punished myself for years, consciously and unconsciously, because I felt responsible for the death of my mother.

I didn't only feel responsible for her death because I wasn't there to stop it, but I felt responsible and guilty because a few months prior to her death, she had complained to me about chest pains. She explained that she wanted to see the cardiologist but wanted me to accompany her. As I got older, my mom no longer seemed to need me to accompany her to medical appointments. Therefore, it was a surprise to me that she wanted me to accompany her this time. At that time, I was in college and working, which left me with little time to myself. She mentioned the appointment one to two more times until it seemed that she had accepted that I probably wasn't going to accompany her. I chose not to accompany her because I had been desensitized by all of my mother's previous physical and mental health conditions. I stopped having much of a reaction whenever she told me that she was experiencing a new symptom because I just felt as though it was something more to add to her extensive list of ailments. I chose not to accompany her because I was strict and rigid regarding my work and school schedule. I didn't miss class or work unless there was an extraneous circumstance or if I had a planned vacation; anything in between just didn't make the cut. Fast forward to when I learned that my mother died of a massive heart attack. I felt like it was me. I had killed my own mother.

In choosing to put everything in front of her, I had contributed to her not going to see the cardiologist for the symptoms that she was experiencing. Although the massive heart attack was caused by two of her medications that were found to have counteracted each other, I still held myself responsible for her death. At the time, I couldn't see it any other way, and when I uttered the words and expressed my guilt to others, it felt so true and real. During this time, I experienced life very differently.

One of the many realizations that I have experienced with my mother's death is that everything that once meant something becomes nothing at some point. As confusing as it sounds, what I mean is that in life, we tend to give value and priority to things and situations that, in the long run, don't truly make up our lives. Whether it is our dream job, house, car, clothes, or whatever other external attachments we form, it all means nothing without the people who mean the most to us. It wasn't until my mom passed away that I felt and was conscious of how much she truly meant to me. Despite the turmoil, despite the not-so-pleasant times, she was and always will be my mother. A mother that I knew did the best she could with what she had at the time. It wasn't until she died that I was able to see life from her lens. I didn't understand when she would say that in a room full of people, she felt alone. During that time, I took it personally because through all of her struggles, I was always present, and it seemed that my presence wasn't enough to make her feel as though she had someone and wasn't, in fact, alone.

That's the thing about life; we become so self-involved and believe that everything that happens around us and how people treat us always has to do with us. Through the pain that death brings forth, I became aware that the way we act and react to one another has to do more with ourselves and the internal battles we may be facing. Someone who is feeling sad and hopeless may view the world from a lens of sadness and hopelessness. Therefore, the way they act and react towards people may be a projection of their emotional and mental states. It wasn't until my mother died that I was able to understand that this was the lens through which she viewed the world. She viewed the world as a place of pain, sadness, and loneliness. All my mother wanted was to feel connected, but like so many of us, she didn't know how to express that and didn't know how to ask for help. Instead, often, she would react out of impulse based on her emotional and mental state of being, whether it was from a state of anger, pain, or sadness.

After the loss of my mother, I have been able to experience a different level of compassion towards myself and others. There are times when we can become so involved with doing that we forget to simply be. I was reminded recently that I am a human BEING and not a human DOER. It took someone to point this out for me to realize how I had been systematically living all this time. I have lived a life whereby my insecurities and fears led me to act in a way that didn't reflect my worth. In a trance of desperation and in fear of experiencing abandonment, I learned to do and do and keep doing for people so that I remained useful to them for as long as I could. I continued doing so that there was a purpose for people to keep me in their lives. I was one of those people who often felt used. But how could I have been used if I was freely and voluntarily giving myself away? I learned that, in essence, I tried to buy the love that I yearned to receive from my mother. I learned that I imposed the brokenness that I felt onto others and expected others to fill that void that haunted me for so many years. Through death, I realized that we often forget to live and instead act like a robot or on autopilot rather than in a human and intentional way. We forget that in the same way we have our own struggles, there are millions of people around us facing their own internal battles. With this, death shifted my perspective into being more present and observant of those around me. It allowed me to feel more connected with my surroundings and the people that I came across. There have been several times when, just looking at someone, I could tell that they were struggling. Because I understood what it was like to silently struggle, there were times when I would ask individuals if they wanted a hug. Not because they told me anything but because I could see in their eyes, in their spirit, that they were in some level of pain. A simple hug proved to be powerful enough to transform an individual's state of being at the time. A hug translated into connection, comfort, support, and being acknowledged that someone saw them and cared about what they were experiencing. Death awoke the eyes of my heart and soul to see what had always been in front of me, but I couldn't see before.

With death, I understood that we are not defined by our jobs, accomplishments, or material wealth. External things are inconsistent and, therefore, place us in a rat race of always having to chase after the next promotion, achievement, and greater wealth. If we know that external items can't provide us with long-term happiness, satisfaction, and peace, then why do we place so much value and priority on them?

Prior to my mother's death and even shortly after, I found myself feeling unfulfilled and empty. I identified so heavily with who I was as a student and a worker that I blindly thought that the way I was going to get out of my "unhappiness" was by getting the highest education possible, which would then lead me to a higher-paying job. With enough education and wealth, I would finally be happy, right? Wrong! I learned these were band-aids that I tried to place on my deep wounds that reopened every so often. As soon as they would reopen, I would immediately try to put on another band-aid and continue masking the internal agony that I was experiencing.

With death, I agonized more. I agonized to the extent that I never imagined possible. Ironically enough, it was through that intense amount of agony that I was able to see myself for who I really was: a soul who was hurting. A hurting soul who had lost her way and didn't know how to return to her home. A hurting soul who had been conditioned to think, feel, and act according to a certain standard that oftentimes indicated that her emotions, her experience, and her thoughts were not valid. A hurting soul who learned to mistrust herself and others. A hurting soul who learned that she wasn't enough as she was and therefore had to do until there was no more doing left. A hurting soul who learned that happiness was only permissible for some, but for some reason, she was not part of the select few. A hurting soul who learned to be in control, and any lack of control would signify her own failure. A hurting soul who worried and felt stress more often than times when she felt at ease and carefree. A hurting soul who learned that she had to be the bigger person from a young age and that at that same young age, she had to always be the one to know better.

With Mom's death, I died too, but this was only one of the many deaths that I already had endured with her. Most were not physical deaths; in fact, the main physical death was my mother's death, while the rest were the deaths of me; the deaths of who I was, who I was supposed to be, who I wanted to be, and who I forced myself to be. All of those versions of me were countless efforts of me trying to be who they wanted me to be, who they felt comfortable with me being, and who they thought served them a purpose for me to be. Through death, I learned that none of those versions were all me.

Death brings forth a permanence like nothing else. And it is the understanding of the permanence of death that has allowed me to take life a little less seriously and value my interactions and connections with people much more. I now take all of my paid time off from work without thinking twice. I now make my family and loved ones a priority before work. I now understand that enjoying the time away from my daily responsibilities is very important. Now, I am not saying work is not important because it allows us to make a living and pay for the things we need. What I am saying is that work can NOT come before people, before those you love and care about. Work can NOT stand in the way of you living because before you know it, you will blink, and your life will have passed you by.

Through death, I was also fortunate enough to uncover my passion or, as some may call it, "my calling." My grief experience, as raw and intense as it has been, has allowed me to see firsthand what we as a people lack. We lack connection. We lack understanding. We lack education and awareness of the unknown and the uncomfortable. Many times, my grief made those around me feel uncomfortable, and it was then that I learned to silence my screams and agony. While I am very far from completing my mission, I have set out to give a voice to the voiceless. I have set out to give a face to the pain that so many experience and don't know how to verbalize. I have set out to normalize the "abnormality" that many see in a person's grief experience.

After the loss of Mom, I made several decisions. I made the decision to argue less and listen more. I made the decision to not leave for tomorrow what I can do today. I made the decision to love more wholeheartedly and appreciate the simple things that, at times, we can take for granted. I made the decision to be more present with people and to speak with an open heart.

A million times, I wished for my mother to be here with me again and to see her one last time. It wasn't until many years later that I was able to accept that it was her time to go. She had left me and my brothers with what was necessary at the time. From that point on, it was up to us how we shaped and lived our lives. Through the pain and the darkness, we learned how to smile again, to have hope again, to live again. That's the thing about life and death; both can rip you apart while putting you back together simultaneously.

Through death, I realized that we are all narrating our lives the way we see it at the time, and it may not always hold a full picture of what our lives actually are. I learned that depending on your perception, you can see things as they are or how you would like them to be. Therefore, if you carry on with the perception that people will always abandon you, you will always find evidence that will validate your story.

While it took me a long time to release and forgive myself for the guilt that I carried in relation to my mom and her death, I finally realized that I wasn't God. As comical as that may sound, I held on to the notion of having to be in control and anticipate life before it happened, as if I were God. Who did I think I was? Life was going to happen regardless of what I did, felt, and thought. So, it didn't matter that I would have called my mom that morning of April 6, 2011. It didn't matter if I had accompanied her to a cardiologist appointment. Because life was and will continue to happen without our consent. There have been countless people that I have spoken to over the years who have said that if they lost their mothers, they would also die with them. I, too, was one of them at one point, but my mother's death taught me that while the pain of grief and loss can consume our everyday existence, somehow and someway, we manage to survive each moment.

Death taught me that life is nothing but a dream, and one day, we will all wake up. Right now is what matters. The people are what matters. Everything else is just a bonus.

I had to experience death for myself to truly tap into this insight about myself, life, and loss. Would I have preferred to gain this insight without my mom dying? Sure. But again, things happen on their own timing. And it has been through my own timing that I have been able to start my own healing process. No one was able to rush me into healing or rush me out of my grief. I've learned that my grief is something that I will always carry because I will always miss my mom. But just because I miss my mom doesn't mean I have to continue suffering. The years of questioning, pain, and grief have allowed me to shed the layers of myself that I perhaps would not have been able to shed before. No one is ever truly ready to lose someone they love, but it is a journey that we will all, at some point, have to experience.

Interestingly enough, every day, I now feel more connected with my mom even though she is not physically present. I truly believe that she wasn't able to help me fully from the physical realm, but she has worked overtime for me in the spiritual realm. I know she is with me every single day and will continue to be with me for the rest of my life. And for that, I will always be grateful and love her for being my mom. Mother of mine, you have taught me that I am enough just the way I am.

CONCLUSION TO BOOK ONE

In trying to find ways to conclude book one, I came across writer's block, fear, and expectations. How could I write an ending for something that was still in progress? I wrote the words, but as I reread them, I cringed and knew they weren't me. It wasn't me, and it was just words put together in order to check a box for the things that needed to be completed. I knew that I was in my head and needed to just get out in order to allow the process to be. How many times have you come across something that was important for you and felt flooded with fear and doubt?

That was me until I finally let go of what it was supposed to look and sound like and simply allowed myself to be. It was a Sunday afternoon when I was searching through my laptop documents to find a picture to send someone. As I clicked through the folders, I came across a folder titled "Mom." I didn't quite remember what was inside this folder, so I opened it. In it were two files: a picture of my dogs taken days after my mom passed away and a letter that I had written to my mom on January 11, 2020.

I vaguely remember the actual content of the letter, but I knew overall what it was about. It was a letter that I had agreed to write as a way of expressing what I wished I could say to her but couldn't after she died. For years, people have insisted that I needed to move on and let go. And for years, I insisted that I didn't need to do a damn thing. There was a lot of resistance and anger that came up for me every time I was told this because I simply could not conceptualize what moving on or letting go looked or felt like. How was I supposed to move on from something that hasn't stopped hurting? How was I supposed to let go of my mom? How was I supposed to let go of the person who brought me into this world?

These words and concepts disturbed me for quite some time, and I usually became very defensive when it was brought up in conversation. After a while, I just got so sick of people telling me how I should or shouldn't be feeling and even how I should be processing my grief that I stopped trying to talk about it with anyone.

There are a select number of people, however, that I've been able to have these kinds of conversations without feeling guarded or defensive. That is because I know that these people have always given me the space and time to process things on my time and not theirs. These people have been a blessing in my life because I could count on them to not judge me or make me feel like the shittiest person to walk this earth. They've met me with love, compassion, comfort, empathy, and warmth throughout my entire journey, no matter how dark it has gotten. One of these people has been my mentor, Damaris, who I am eternally grateful to have in my life. We met when I was fifteen years old and have intentionally continued being in each other's lives. She was one of the first people that I felt safe enough to open up to about my life. At fifteen, there was a lot that I was struggling with and holding inside. This was around the same time that I started to write this book. With every experience I shared with her and with every thought I verbalized, she never once told me how I should or shouldn't be feeling. If anything, she validated me and helped me to feel like less of an alien in my own grief experience.

Okay, now let's go back to the letter that I wrote to my mom. It was January 2020, and I had met up with Damaris to catch up on our lives and anything new that we had going on. After our usual chitchat, we shifted to a conversation about what it meant to "let go." I explained to her that I didn't understand what "letting go" meant, looked, or felt like, much less how to actually do it. During this time, all she did was listen. I elaborated on my conflicting feelings surrounding the topic of letting go and shared with her that I didn't want to let go of my mom, even though people felt that I needed to in order to heal from the loss of her. For such a long time, I have felt as though the world saw me as someone who was broken and needed to be fixed. Damaris never made me feel like I was broken because she loved me for what I have been throughout our entire relationship. On my best days and my worst days, she has seen me for me.

As I talked and shared my thoughts and feelings, she met me with understanding and validation for my frustrations regarding the notion of "letting go." For once, I wasn't guarded or felt like I had to defend my point to someone about this. For once, I felt relieved. I felt heard and understood. For once, I felt like someone was present with me and not trying to push me in the direction that they felt was right for me. For once, I felt connected. With the sense of relief came the flood of emotions of truly wanting to learn how to look at my life experiences with my mom and myself and not have to constantly feel this pain. I realized that I didn't want to continue living life as a death sentence or living it like a burden and chore. I wanted to be free from this pain and to let go of my internal suffering.

Damaris looked at me and explained that letting go didn't have to have one set meaning to it or look one set way. Letting go could look and feel differently for everyone. She helped me understand that the notion of letting go didn't mean that I had to leave my mother behind; it meant that in due time, part of my healing process would be to revisit those parts of my life that brought me so much pain, to process them for what they were, and let go of the bond that I had with that pain. I no longer lived in those places and had to bring that awareness to my mind, spirit, and body. Letting go meant letting go of the idea and illusion of how I wanted my life with my mom to be and learning to accept my experiences with her for what they were. During the good and not-so-good times, learning to acknowledge that she and I did the best we could with what we had at the time was what letting go could look like for me.

For once, I was open to this notion of letting go because I felt that it was tailored to my experience and me. I felt that I could finally look and think about letting go without wanting to scream or feel angry. Damaris gave me a gift that day. She helped me to understand that I was and always will be the author of my story. I get to write and live my own story and things as they work for me. She helped me understand that my life may not look and feel the same as yours, and that is okay. I felt less ashamed and less alienated because I was okay with my life looking differently from others. That's what makes our stories ours to tell. We all share commonalities and differences, but at the end of the day, we all walk our own individual paths. No story is right or wrong because it is YOUR story.

After having this conversation with Damaris, I wanted to know more about this concept of letting go and its practicality. If this was something that I could tailor to myself, then I wanted to learn about how I could embark on this journey. Damaris shared a few suggestions and ideas on how I could start to process my experiences without adding the pressure of time or expectation over them. The idea that resonated the most with me was to write a letter to my mom, expressing anything and everything that I've ever wanted to say to her, both in the past and present. She warned me that this would probably come with difficulty because of the emotions that could come up but that it was all part of the process. And again, she reiterated the fact that when these emotions became too much to process, I could always walk away and come back to it when I felt ready. Over time, I realized that it felt like a natural response to run away from my unpleasant emotions and reactions to experiences. However, it has been through the discomfort that I was able to gain the most insight about myself. The answers to our questions are all within us, but sometimes, facing those decisions makes us feel uneasy because of what outcomes it may bring forth.

The final step to writing the letter was to go to the cemetery where my mom was buried and read it out loud in front of her grave. I was open to this idea and was curious to see how the experience unfolded. My only hope going into it was that it could help me lighten my load and start to put down the years of repressed emotions and pain that I had been carrying for so long. Notice how I said put down; I say put down the emotions and pain that I had been carrying because oftentimes, we are told or we think that we have to either resist or not feel the emotions that come up with our experiences. Putting down my emotions and pain meant that I would sit with them, hear them out, validate them for what they were, and put them down with love and compassion rather than meeting them with shame, judgment, and criticism. All of our emotions and coping mechanisms serve a purpose during a period. And there comes a point when we hold on to these coping mechanisms past the needed timeframe. The coping mechanisms we once needed to survive are there to help us but not to stay with us forever.

I started to write the letter on January 11th and finished it on January 26th. This was a big step for me because, with every moment that I went back to the letter, I felt that I was giving myself grace in knowing that I didn't have to put the pressure of time or expectations on this process. I could just allow it to flow however it came up during whatever time it needed. I share with you here the letter that I wrote to my mom:

January 11, 2020

Dear Mother:

As I write you this letter, I have no idea where to begin. Since you left in 2011, I have felt a void that, while it has been there before you passed, has only enlarged after you left. I want to start off by first saying thank you. Thank you for being my mother. Thank you for giving me my two brothers. Thank you for doing the best you could with what you had to offer. It's funny because I remember you would often say that in a room full of people, you still managed to feel alone. I didn't get it at the time, and honestly, during that time, I thought you were just being dramatic. But I get it now, and I started getting it soon after you left.

With you, I felt connected. I felt I had a sense of purpose, even though there was usually turmoil and chaos surrounding you. Anything else simply felt unnatural. That's the thing; life without you seems unnatural. In losing you, I lost who I was. Recently, I've been upset with you because I feel that you left and forgot to take me with you. More often than not, I feel like I don't belong here. I feel that no matter how well things may go, at the end of the day, everything is for nothing. I feel that as much as I try to push and move forward, nothing seems to fill me or make me feel connected.

To say that I've grown tired is an understatement. And it's not as much physically tiring as it is emotionally and spiritually. I've thought about my death more than I've thought about living. I feel ungrateful because I know what and who I have, and for some reason, it's not enough. I think that I haven't gone through with offing myself in the hopes that one day I will wake up differently, and I also consider the pain I would leave behind. But that, too, is all fading because I am simply tired.

Again, I learned that death could be an escape route from life and pain through you and all the different times I helped you clean your bloodied veins or helped you throw up the excess medication that you tried to overdose on. It's like you wanted to die but at the same time wanted someone to save you. Mom, I saved you so many times, and yet this one time, I couldn't. I often thought about the day you left and visualized all of the different possibilities that could have happened that would have kept you here, yet the possibility of you dying happened. I will be honest when I tell you that I visualized and felt your death long before it happened. Ever since I was seven years old and you started to have your surgeries, I always grieved your death before the surgery because I didn't understand that you would be able to come out alive. I would tell my friends that my mom was out to die, and then you didn't, which would give me a temporary sense of relief. But then I developed the urgency to care for you as you would come home, appearing fragile and in pain. I absorbed a lot of your pain, and how I wished at that time I could've taken it all. I didn't want you to suffer, but you did. And thus came the thought that I had to help and take care of people who were in pain or some kind of trouble.

I enjoy helping people, but is that really just me hiding behind their problems simply because I can't seem to confront my own? At times, I've taken in their problems and situations as though they were my own. What is my problem? My problem is you, Mom. You built me up to be a fucking leach that doesn't know how to function without chaos. You taught me to be silent even when I was living in hell. You taught me to feel like I wasn't enough because nothing that I ever did for you was enough. You wanted from me what you couldn't give yourself, and now I want from others what you failed to teach me to give to myself. I feel worthless and invisible. And while I do have the support of people, nothing feels like enough. Sound familiar? You taught me to be you, and now I feel that I am you, with the exception that I have some knowledge and awareness. But for some reason, all the knowledge and awareness can't seem to break down the perceptions, habits, and behaviors that you ingrained in me.

Of course, I accept my own responsibility in the matter and understand that I have a choice to be different, but how can I be different without feeling like I am not being true to myself. You were my purpose. You gave me purpose. And now that you are not here, what is my purpose? I've had to entertain myself, my time, and my mind with activities and school to the point of exhaustion just to try to fill the void. And yet, the void still remains. The funny thing is that the void has been there long before you were gone. You co-created that void with me because you left, and I still had the hope that you would be the mother I needed and that, finally, you would see me and tell me that I am enough. The emptiness and need to compensate and go above and beyond stems from me feeling little in your eyes. No matter how much or how little I did, in your eyes, it felt to equate to the same. And now I am left yearning for the acknowledgment of others in hopes that with them, I will feel like I am enough.

The reality is I feel so fucked up, and I feel like there's nothing that I do to change that. As many steps forward as I have taken over the years, I still feel that void, that emptiness. There are times I feel guilty for being alive and taking the place of people who want to live and can't. So many times, I have said I don't want to be here anymore; I remember imploring God to take me when you were still here. And sadly enough, I still have those thoughts. The years of fighting, chaos, drama, and being abandoned by you led me to feel like no one loved me. Because love wasn't any of that which you showed me. With you, I constantly had to fight and fight and fight until there was no more fighting to be done. And all for what I ask myself sometimes. There was a lifelong torment, sadness, anger, resentment, fear, anxiety, and worry that I should be anticipating the worst outcome. You taught me to anticipate when you started to harm yourself. With you, I learned deductive reasoning and to observe people's patterns in order to understand and anticipate their next move, their next words, and their thought processes. Do you *know how exhausting that is? While it has protected me in several situations, it has also destroyed me and my potential to be happy because I feel that I have to experience the loss before it even happens, as if that helps the pain feel any less.*

Mom, you fucked me up, yet I wouldn't trade you for the world. You felt like I never loved you as much as I loved Dad, yet at one point, we were all in your corner, trying to help you and support you the best way we could. But you couldn't see it. And at times, it's even harder for me to see it. I've fought so hard to be everything opposite of you, and as I sit writing this letter, I feel that I've turned out to be you. I am, at times, tormented by my existence like you were, and I just wake up at times with the feelings of wanting to be over. And yet I've stuck it out this far; that makes me either a masochist, coward, or brave. It's all about perspective.

While I was living the hell with you, I hated you. I resented you. I even wished for you to finally die. But after a while, those feelings subsided, and I saw a part of you that I don't know if I have ever had the chance to experience. Your presence taught me to feel fear because I never knew what would happen when you were around, but this time it felt different. Your aura felt light, and I saw the light in your eyes. I was able to see you, Mom, for the first time in years. And as with all good things in life, Mom, this was all short-lived. Then you left.

Life is about perspective, right? I could say that this was your way of redeeming yourself, preparing yourself, and allowing yourself to forgive and be forgiven. I don't think I ever got to tell you that I have forgiven you, and Mom, I forgive you because throughout all the shit you put my brothers and me through, I know that inside were just feelings and thoughts that you couldn't control and would lead to your impulsive and maladaptive behavior. Mom, I know that you simply did the best you could. You taught us how to be self-sufficient and self-reliant. You taught us to not care what others had to say or think, even though I know it killed you when people would cast you as the black sheep. This is the reason I felt that I had to defend you against the world; they didn't understand your pain, especially during the last time that you were admitted into the psych unit, based on your history, not on anything current.

At 20 years old, the doctors and nurses initially didn't want to take me seriously, but that was short-lived once I laid out all of the cards on the table about you and the logic and evidence that helped paint a different picture of you. I remember feeling angry because I knew people judged you as being crazy. But crazy or not, you were my mother, and I am proud to have you as my mother. Thank you, Mom, for all that you gave me and did for me. I still remember the nights I had my usual stomach pains, and you would stay up all night with me in your arms, rocking me back and forth until the pain subsided. I know that through it all, you were still inside there, even if I couldn't see you at times.

Mom, I am sorry for the pain that you suffered. I am sorry for people's disdain towards you. I am sorry for all the times you felt that you were not enough because you were and are enough to me. I am sorry for all the times that you felt alone, even when I was there. I am sorry for it all. And now, at my greatest attempt to change my own mold, I have to forgive myself for all that I've put myself through: the pain, suffering, neglect, and abuse. I've involved myself in situations where

I allowed myself to be treated poorly and not with the love that I deserve. I know I deserve better, but I don't feel that way, which has led me to tolerate a lot of things that I should have never entertained in the first place. I need to forgive myself for having to kill that little girl I once was to become what you needed me to be.

Mom, I want you to be at peace. As much as I have been holding on to you and your memory, which fills me with pain, I know that I have to let go. I've tried to let you go several times, but for some reason, the words didn't line up with the thoughts or actions.

Mom, I love you, and I want you to be ok wherever you are. You now have a different purpose for living, and so do I. I just ask that in your role, purpose, transition or whatever you call it, you know that I've always loved you and always will love you. You were my purpose, and now I have to find a new one, but in living out my new purpose, everyone will know that I am my mother's daughter, your daughter, and my one true love.

Sincerely,

Your daughter

1/26/2020

After writing this letter, Damaris accompanied me to the cemetery, where I read it out loud in front of my mother's grave. A mixture of emotions came to my mind while I was writing and reading this letter. I felt a lightness in my body that I had not really felt before because I finally felt like I could say what I truly felt, thought, and experienced without having my fears and judgment present.

After reading the letter, I set it on fire and watched it turn into ashes. I didn't want the pain that came from these experiences to continue writing my story. I didn't want to feel like a prisoner of my past experiences. I wanted to learn what it meant and felt like embracing all of it and understanding that it has all been a part of the process of getting to know myself in all the different facets of my life. Sometimes, we don't know what we are capable of until we experience something that highlights that part of us.

I used to look at my experiences and remember how I felt like I died a bit more with every single one of them. I used to look at this with sadness because I felt that there would come a point when all of me would finally die. Today, I acknowledge the parts of me that have died and continue to die, but not just from the lens of sadness. I've realized and understood that through our experiences, we may lose parts of ourselves, and that is okay. It's okay because those parts have served their purpose during the time we have needed them and have given way for the other parts of ourselves to come in and continue to guide us throughout our life's journey.

My journey up to this point has also helped me realize how damaging it can be to our sense of well-being to not be able to say how we truly feel out loud without the fear of judgment and shame. It was when I realized that behind people's shame and judgment of the way I was experiencing my own grief was a projection of their own discomfort. We don't grow up in a society that is comfortable with having conversations related to loss or death because those are considered to be "negative" topics. It is almost as though people think that talking openly about death will somehow attract it into your life. Let me tell you that it doesn't! My experience with loss and everything that came with it pushed me to create the change that I wanted to see in the world. I founded Life after Loss in 2019 in an effort to help create a safe space for many people like myself who have felt alone and disconnected in their grief experience. My mission and purpose are to normalize conversations around death and the grief experience. I am fighting to end the stigma of what society thinks our grief should look like because there is no right or wrong way to grieve. There is only YOUR way. You can check out my website, www.LifeafterLoss.co, for more information.

A note to myself for when things start to feel heavy again:

Lindsay,

You are doing the best you can right now, and that is enough. Even if you're doing nothing right now, I promise you it is enough. You, my love, are a beautiful and majestic creature that is fully deserving of love. You are enough. You have always been enough. I know you have felt and experienced a great deal of pain and loss throughout your life. You've built an exterior that, from the outside, seems solid, put together, at times distant and guarded, motivated, driven, and focused. But I know on the inside, it still feels hard. It feels hard, and you're still getting used to acknowledging that out loud. You know you have many people in your life who love and support you. But for some reason, you still find it hard to feel alive and connected.

The remnants of your past experiences still linger. They linger because you still hold on to them tightly with the fear that letting them go would be like letting go of your mom. You experienced a lot with her. You loved her. You hated her. Yet, you would never trade her for anything else in this world. As your layers continue to peel back, remember that they will only come off when you are ready. Let them come off with appreciation and love for the many ways they have served you. There is no rush. There is no timeline. Silence the white noise that prevents you from listening to your heart and spirit.

You started this journey of writing this book with a lot of ambition, goals, and vision. Three parts, twenty-two chapters by December 2020. It didn't happen. Not because you failed or did something wrong but because your story is still developing. What you needed to write right now has been written. The parts of your life and story that you needed to share with the world have been shared. This is enough. You will continue to write your story, and it will be one hell of a story, not because of what people say or any kind of recognition but because, despite it all, you did this for that little girl who felt like she had to silence her pain. That little girl still struggles from time to time, but she has come so far from where she started.

You will always have a voice.

This is my story. Thank you for joining me on this journey. I hope that when you close this book, you, too, will know that your story is also worth telling and powerful. Sending a big hug to everyone currently trying to make sense of this life.

Thank you.

www.ingramcontent.com/pod-product-compliance
Lightning Source LLC
Chambersburg PA
CBHW021108130626
46554CB00002B/590